After Basho

Matsuo Munefusa - Basho (1644–1694)

Who is to tell the tale
of those days in Budapest
when dead horses were skinned
and sliced for meat,
if not an anguished father
burying his son?

Who is to tell the tale
of the Chatham bellbird
whose dawn-greeting songs
are no longer heard,
if not a sheep herder
dreaming of green pastures?

Who is to tell the tale
of our bliss-seeking lives
spent in a breathless rush
to reach distant stars,
if not a fraught fisherman
buffeted by gales?

"...not biographical memory,
but an emotional memory of climates..."

(Bruno Schulz, 1892–1942)

BY THE SAME AUTHOR

POETRY

Taxi! Taxi! (2008)
Maitai River Press

CD

Born in Budapest
with music by Gábor Tolnay (2010)

Love & War In The Yurt
with music by Gábor Tolnay and Simon Williams (2014)
Maitai River Press

BUDAPEST GIRL

BUDAPEST GIRL

an immigrant confronts the past

PANNI PALÁSTI

MAITAI RIVER PRESS

www.maitairiverpress.co.nz

Published 2015
by Maitai River Press

Third printing

ISBN 978-0-473-34371-2

A catalogue record for this book is available
from the National Library of New Zealand.

With grateful acknowledgement by the author for assistance received through the Mentor Programme and the CompleteMS manuscript assessment programme, which are administered and run by the New Zealand Society of Authors (PEN Inc) and supported by Creative New Zealand.

Cover photograph by Veres, Budapest
Design by Suzanne North

Printed by The Copy Press, Nelson, New Zealand. www.copypress.co.nz

Introduction

This book is not fiction. Every event truly happened. Every character is a real person, either dead or still alive. In the rare instances when I rely upon my imagination I do say so.

A table of contents is missing because of the sheer number of chapters, some of them not more than a few lines, and because the chapter titles do not necessarily correspond to the contents of a particular memory, but state instead my current, and possibly more adult, attitude to the content. For a semblance of order, I numbered the chapters.

What I have been trying to do is to suggest the peculiar flamboyance of memories as they surface keeping to their own dynamic timetable.

The vintage photos scattered throughout were either taken by unknowns in the early 20th century and handed down through generations, or were taken by my father and myself later.

Who Was Who

ANYU

Anyu was my mother, Vilma Palkó, born in the village of Püski in 1902, daughter of Grandma, Etel Markó, adopted daughter of József Palkó. Birth father unknown.

APU

Apu was my father, born László Szilágyi in Budapest in 1903. He later changed his surname to his pen name: Palásti. His mother was Gizella Petyán, my Ómama. His reprobate father was Miksa Szilágyi, who died before I was born.

GRANDMA

Grandma, Anyu's mother, was born in the village of Püski in 1882, the oldest of seven children to János Markó and Katalin Ekker. Beside Vilma, my mother, she raised a son, Feri, my hunchback uncle. She also raised me because Anyu had to go to work to support us before the war, because Apu could not get a job.

ÓMAMA

Ómama, my father's mother Gizella Petyán was born somewhere in Hont County, now situated in Slovakia, in 1873. I have no record of her birthplace and don't know who were her parents. She survived the war in the Budapest Ghetto, but died soon afterwards.

ÓPAPA

My father's father Miksa Szilágyi lived from 1869 to 1930. He changed his name from Sonnenfeld to Szilágyi in the 1890s in Budapest. In spite of searching, I could not find out where he was born. He left Ómama to marry a rich woman, so neither she nor my father talked about him. His grave can be found in Rákoskeresztúr.

GRANDPA

His name was József Palkó. I could not find out when he was born or where. He married Grandma and adopted my mother when she was nine years old, thereby changing her surname from Markó to Palkó. I was a toddler when he fell off his fiacre and died, so I can only remember his grave Grandma and I visited every year at All Saints' Day.

TERIKE

As a child, I called her Terike, using her diminutive nickname, not her official name, Markó Teréz. She was my second cousin, born in 1928 in Püski to Aunt Terus and Uncle Pista, the brother of Grandma. Of all my relatives she was the closest to me. The five years of difference in our age made no difference to our friendship.

UNCLE PISTA

He was born in 1888, six years after Grandma. During the First World War he was drafted into the Austro-Hungarian army and was taken prisoner in Russia where he spent years trying to escape. He learned Russian and watched the revolution there. He married Aunt Terus when he arrived back in Püski.

AUNTIE TERUS

She was the mother of Terike, as well as Géza, her firstborn, who perished in the war. Her other children were Pisti, Katus and Feri, all of whom were part of my childhood during my summer holidays in the village. She accompanied my mother to search for my father among the doomed marching towards German concentration camps in 1944.

AUNTIE ILONKA

Grandma's youngest sister, Anyu's aunt, who was two years younger than my mother. On the way to Püski, I often stayed in her house while her husband was away in the Russian front. He froze to death there, as I have described in a poem trying to come to terms with the waste and sorrow of wars.

AUNTIE KATUS

Terike's older sister, second child of Aunt Terus. She stayed with us in Budapest for a while learning city housekeeping from Grandma. She was in her teens then, and Grandma proved to be a tough teacher. I recall her slapping Katus when she forgot to mend a run in her stocking and used a safety pin to stop it.

AUNTIE ZITA

She was the beautiful wife of Oscar, a friend and colleague of my father and a close friend of Anyu. Theirs was a similar match to that of my parents, Oscar being Jewish and Zita Roman Catholic. As a child, I loved the taste of their eggnog and wanted to marry Oscar.

AUNTIE BÖZSI

A diminutive woman who was a cousin of Apu. She lived in Paris before the war. She taught me French when I was 12 and implanted in my mind a desire for travel and a love of French authors like Zola, Stendhal, Flaubert and Balzac.

VICA

Vica was my closest friend and my everyday playmate from age two to twelve. She lived in a house attached to ours, and the yard and buildings were our playground. She was the daughter of Mr Bauer, the assistant foreman in the Adolf Baum factory, while her grandfather was the chief foreman, living in the same house.

MR BAUER

During the war Vica's father, Mr Bauer was the boss of the air raid shelter and the house. He treated me well, but I was afraid of him because of his pro-Hitler stance when we were hiding Apu from the Gestapo.

MR KELEMEN

He was the concierge in charge of the gate, the yard, the flowers and the grass. He was also in charge of letting you in and out after ten o'clock at night and searching for stolen goods in the satchels of factory workers. He knew everything that happened in the house.

KITTY

The only child of young Mr and Mrs Baum. She lived on the top floor and had her own separate room full of toys. When she invited me, I loved to play with her miniature villages and farm animals, her doll collection and the trains that ran around twisting tracks on the carpet.

OLD MRS BAUM

Wife of old Mr Baum, who started the factory. She was Kitty's grandmother, and the cause of my first brush with diabetes.

ANTONIA

The assistant concierge. A large and mostly quiet woman who emptied the rubbish boxes for all the flats and mopped the stairs.

PAULA

The maid of old Mrs Baum. Her room was facing our window. I liked to watch her shake dust rags on the corridor. She was killed on the street during the 1956 revolution.

MR AND MRS ROSTOS

An elegant couple living above us. When Jews were ordered out of the house and they had to go, they gave me some beautiful toys left behind by their only daughter. I enjoyed riding her scooter in between air raids.

VALI AND BABA

Vali and Baba are my oldest friends from gymnasium years. I still see them both whenever I go to Budapest. With Baba we agree about everything except daily politics. It is an enduring friendship. With Vali, we are soul mates in every way.

ZSOLDOS

Apu's best friend and role model. They met in the early 1920s, and their friendship continued in Berlin and in Hollywood, where Apu visited him in the 1970s.

HITLER

A German leader who liked to shout on newsreels and who started the Second World War. He caused much suffering, and I hatched a lot of secret plans to get rid of him.

HORTHY

Hungary's governor and Regent of the Kingdom of Hungary from 1920 to 1944. He liked to be photographed riding a big white horse and was too late to break with Hitler and to stop fighting on the losing German side.

MRS KENDE

A retired teacher and our next door neighbour who poked her nose into Grandma's pots and pans every day, wanting to know what she cooked. She let me taste her own cooking though. She survived the war in the Budapest ghetto.

The names above

I can't name them all. So the list remains incomplete.

Sometimes I feel obliged to change a name to protect the living, those who may take umbrage if I tell the truth about the past. Faced with the choice between telling and naming I have chosen to tell but alter a few names.

The instinct to protect progeny prevails.

Prologue

Decades of delay

A stranger can ask a question that changes the way you see your life.

"Why did you wait for six decades to write this memoir?"

I wanted to forget the war.

"Why don't you mention until page 74 that your father was Jewish?"

Why? Maybe because as a child I was afraid of being branded a Jew.

The questions of this casual visitor from London unsettled me enough to look at my life from a new angle, to recognise my excuses and to step over them.

I was born in 1933, the year Hitler rose to power.

It was not an auspicious year to be the newborn of a Roman Catholic mother and a Jewish father in Hungary, a country that was still nursing its wounds after a lost war, a failed Communist dictatorship and the impact of the Great Depression. Anti-Semitism was on the rise. As a small child I remained unaware of the workings of the wider world. My parents tried to hide their worries and keep me sheltered in a cocoon of care.

Only in 1940 did I start to notice the perils they faced.

And only now, in my 80s can I see that most of my life I tried hard to evade being thought of as a part Jew. I carried with me the compulsion to shed the past even to America, where I arrived at 23 as a refugee. And I carried it on to peaceful New Zealand where I landed in 1973.

It only happened in 2014 that in the Internet I stumbled upon the right word for my lasting unease.

It is a German word: *Mischling*.

It means mongrel, crossbreed, hybrid, half-caste.

Yes, it took me many decades to deal with this fear that originated in my childhood, the fear that I refused to acknowledge, the urge to swim in the mainstream, to seek a cloudless life.

Only today can I look with calm and rational disdain at the black and white figurines of the Nazi Racial Chart drawn of people with mixed parentage. A white Aryan silhouette next to a blackened Jew: their marriage *Verboten!*

My parents? Not permitted!

My birth? Prohibited!

Their child, a *mischling* "of the first degree", is to be sterilized.

The grey figure of a mongrel next to a white Aryan: my own happy marriage, *Verboten!*

Yes, it took me many decades to sit down and write this memoir.

The Press of Other Lives

Like a leaf of grass
in a dense pasture
I am entwined in the tendrils
of other lives.

My roots tangle
with their roots.
My need for light
shares their need.
My reach for food
meets with their hunger.
I dream their dreams
and drink their tears.

Their face may fade
their cries subside
but they echo,
claim and touch me,
make me swallow
more than I can hold.

Juggling mysteries

I don't know anybody in this photo. I inherited it with stacks of others when my father died almost four decades ago. Because he saved it, I think the small boy could be him. The man, whose hands are resting on his shoulders could be my grandfather, and the big woman standing proudly on the right, could be his wife, my grandmother. The truth is that I am not sure. The other central woman could be anyone, young and fashionable, it could even be Aunt Berta, grandmother's younger sister visiting Budapest from America.

There is nobody left to ask.

My father left me many pictures. They bring back a flood of memories coming in sweeping waves one after another in no discernible order. This memoir obeys the waves, and although I have tried to respect chronology, I often go with the waves instead, submit to the chaos of flashbacks.

Right now, another adamant memory calls.

It makes me jump from this photo circa 1904 to a dark, decisive day in 1956 when I was escaping from Hungary, becoming a refugee, starting my journey as an emigrant.

Crossing in silence

Can you see us move in the dark?
Can you see us lurch like a wounded lizard?
We raise a lolling head towards
the night sky devoid of direction
our body pulses with pain
straining to advance

Do you hear our shoes squelch
old men cough and curse under their breath
and their heavy wives groan at each step they take
hunched under bundles weighing them down

Do you hear the mother
shushing her babe while
her fumbling fingers unbutton her coat
to offer her breast
trying to still her whimpering child

Do you smell our unwashed clothes
soaked in sweat and fear

We are one now
although we don't know each other
thrown together from far frontiers
past allies and past enemies
a rootless huddle
waiting for darkness
for moonless nights to cross the morass
between borders bristling with guards
zigzagging our way across no man's land
towards a promised land
that may
or may not
take us in

1

Going away

Moonlight means danger when you are trying to creep across a border.

You want to disappear, merge with the earth, blend into the sky when you feel searching eyes on your back, eyes turning guns in your direction.

The patrols are vigilant. They don't speak your language, and their orders are clear: nobody is to cross.

This is the last stretch.

The border is straight ahead, that's what the tall man said when he brought us through the trees, before he turned back at the edge of the forest. "You only paid me to bring you this far," he whispered. "Keep going. But when they send up flares, lie down in the snow. Be silent. Don't move. Don't lift your head until the flares go out and it's dark again."

We are left facing a bare stretch of flat land patrolled by a line of Russian tanks. A few days ago twenty of us left Budapest in the back of a truck pretending to be potatoes covered with tattered old potato sacks. We are now diminished to a motley dozen, young and old, men, women and children. Eight have chickened out on the way.

It was not easy to huddle on top of each other whenever a roadside patrol stopped the truck and lifted the tarpaulin to see inside. I can still smell the sacks and the bodies on top of me, a smell no soap can remove.

We trudge on, hoping to reach Austria.

It is a cold December day. Our revolution is crushed. We are on the move.

2

Gene carriers

Looking back at that December day six decades later, I notice a pattern, the pattern of flight.

Could it be passed on through generations? This constant movement away from danger, from war, poverty, hunger or persecution is fed by the hope of finding better pastures, of finding a safe place to raise the next generation.

When my parents fled from Berlin in 1933 to Budapest, did my mother's fears affect me just a few weeks before I was born?

And did my father's ancestors fleeing across Europe and ending up in America like so many in the 19th and 20th centuries, did they follow the same pattern of flight?

Further back, the restless tribes of prehistory, later called Hungarians, moving from east towards west and ending in up in Europe, did they carry the same hunger in their genes?

Now we can find and date the bones to prove that millions of years ago our earliest ancestors left their birthplace in Africa and crossed seas and continents.

We are learning so much, but changing so little.

Yes, I am a migrant.

I am not alone.

Migrants.

Gene carriers.

Gene mixers and gene adapters.

On restless nights I am still heading for borders.

3

Chaff in the whirlwind

My parents left Germany in 1933.

They fled just in time.

Because the Reichstag burned, I was not born in Berlin.

I landed in a wicker laundry basket in Budapest instead.

My life started in Berlin, but my story must reach backwards as far as the Austro-Hungarian Empire in search of my ancestors and as far forward as Aotearoa, New Zealand, where I am still alive.

Where should I start? How should I keep order? I remember how I needed order as a child. I found it in Grandma's kitchen, and I found it in the tennis court.

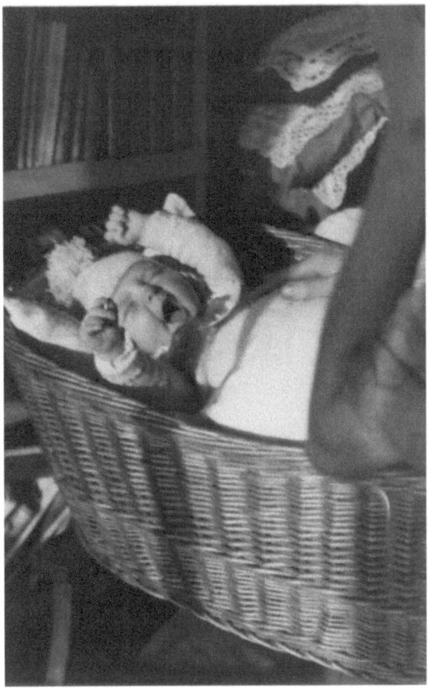

Sunday tennis

How I loved order as a child;
the smell of straight rulers and the
swift needle of the grocer's scale,
the musts of school and the don'ts of church.

And most of all, the tennis court.
Fresh white lines on the raked red clay,
the net cutting it into two
exactly abiding mirror-halves.

Father serves, mother at the net
lobs one right into the corner.
Game, set, match and raspberry soda
through a straw on the wide verandah.

Frog music wafts from a bottomless lake
as we board a yellow streetcar
and glide home where oleanders
bloom in the iron-railed corridors.

We float through the hushed Sunday streets,
the three of us, on cobblestones
still warm, smudged by the setting sun,
content and careless of chaos to come.

*

How old was I on that hushed Sunday? Maybe five, perhaps six.

It is time to start applying the discipline of chronology, to start earlier. To tell the story of the day my parents met.

4

My father's name was László Szilágyi
My mother's was Vilma Palkó

The tennis court by the Budapest Zoo was teeming with men in white hitting white tennis balls over a net. Their volleys seemed to go on and on. Back and forth, back and forth shot the ball with gunshot sharp smacks as the men moved with lightning speed.

She was young, less than 20, a tired typist on her way home after work stopping for a moment to watch. Not the first time. She got off the subway to walk through the park, choosing to take longer to get home, in order to enjoy the fresh air and to see tennis, a sport from another world.

From an affluent world of leisure.

She watched a man leap from the net sending the ball high in the sky behind the back of his opponent, so high that it seemed to be

aimed at the clouds, and when it descended it passed over the tall fence where she was standing. She turned and retrieved it from a lilac bush behind her, swung around and threw it back.

One of the men in white standing behind the fence admiring her energetic lob, asked her whether she played tennis. He offered to teach her.

She said she would think about it.

He loaned her a tennis racket. She bought a length of white cotton and sewed a dress with a short skirt pleated front and back.

Her mother was baffled by her sudden and unbecoming interest in tennis. His mother found every girl the wrong one for her son, especially a *shiksa.*

They met more and more often, on and off the court. He took her to coffee houses, to movies, to the theatre and, in time, to trips around the country when he had assignments to report from provincial towns.

He was a fledgling journalist with high ambitions and a voracious curiosity about the world. When he heard about the intellectual ferment in Berlin and about the careers many Hungarians started to make there, he decided to try his luck.

Preparing to leave Budapest led to arguments.

He was her first love.

For him she was the first serious one, but in spite of his passionate pleas, she couldn't be persuaded to go.

She refused to see him off when he boarded the train to Germany.

He remained undaunted and showered her with love letters. To avoid the eyes of her mother, he addressed them to the law office where she worked.

5

An antique shop in Berlin

A streetlight shot a sickly yellow beam at the shop window and hit a crystal glass. It burst into the colours of the rainbow and danced around the walls of my future father's temporary shelter. "All the relics around me came to life," he used to tell me. "Kept me awake."

I gathered from the flotsam of his notes how poor he had been in Berlin where he often depended on borrowed money cadged from other Hungarians. He made jokes about members of the émigré community, the way they crossed the street to avoid meeting each other and being fleeced.

He couldn't afford to pay rent. So he negotiated with an old antique dealer who allowed him to sleep in his shop. The place was bulging with dark furniture, estate jewellery in glass-topped display boxes and threadbare Persian rugs.

Herr Blum (who had a soft spot for Hungarians due to a short romance with a Hungarian baroness in the 1880s) provided him with a blanket and a pillow beside permission to bed down on an antique chaise longue.

All this luxury was his in exchange for free advertising in his startup periodical, the *Berliner Kurier* of doubtful circulation.

He had to wait every day until the shop closed in the evening. Herr Blum, a lonely widower, had no reason to go home early. Father was obliged to wait on park benches, in hotel lobbies or smoke-filled coffee houses if he had enough change to pay for a cup.

I can see him, tired and coughing in the rain, his head sunk between his shoulders, turning the key in the shop's door and winding his way to the back to collapse on the chaise longue, his designated bed.

Years later he still dreamed about the place, about the dealer, a slight man with a limp and a generous heart, who specialized in rococo furniture and Renaissance revival tables. The chaise longue was too short for his lanky body, forcing him to sleep in the foetal position.

Near his head loomed a serpentine-shaped rococo dresser with drawers adorned by pendulous bronze leaf pulls that he used to stare at before he managed to fall asleep. It was one of his favorite tales about Berlin, and I often asked him to tell it to me again so that I could climb up into his arms and watch him closing his eyes in order to see those pendulous pulls, and I did the same to make me see them as well.

He dreaded the beveled mirrors that reflected the light beams and the fringed lampshades of standing lamps, ghosts of his fevered nights.

That's where he lay when he fell sick with pneumonia.

6

A train to Berlin

As a bona fide foreign correspondent, my father was depending on money from the papers in Budapest. They were not in a hurry to pay a new boy abroad. He phoned, wrote, begged from the distance and lived on promises. When the pay arrived, it was a feast day.

Luckily, he had a girl in Budapest he could send around to collect. Her tentative forays to editorial offices were successful only on rare occasions. She was treated like any pretty girl, as the butt of jokes with sexual overtones. All she achieved most of the time was a promise of payments to be sent directly to Berlin.

Then one day she received a disturbing letter. He was ill. He was desperate and penniless. He needed her.

She packed her best dress and the cardigan her mother knitted for her last Christmas. She bought a train ticket with the money she had saved from the wages earned in the office of a struggling lawyer. She was careful to keep a few *pengős* for Berlin. To buy food, medicine, whatever. Just in case.

The train ride was exciting. Crossing a border meant a lot. It was her first crossing into another world, another language. Her face was

radiant as she stepped off the train in Berlin. She picked him out in the crowd on the platform and her smile faded. He was pale. His face was hollow. He was leaning against a post looking at her with sunken eyes. He was so unsteady, he could hardly lift her suitcase. She let him do it. He needed to save face.

"Tonight it is the antique shop," he said in a rush between coughs, "but soon we can move into a room I've rented in the flat of a widow called Frau Koepfli. It is a decent room with a decent bed and free use of the kitchen. I can't wait for your good Hungarian *gulyás* with *csipetke*."

"I brought you some fresh *zsemle* and *szalámi* and *túró*."

"We can feast tonight on a Biedermeier table and sit on carver chairs," he said, "and I happen to have a bottle of Dreher hidden under an ottoman. To drink with the *szalámi*."

He changed some of the money she handed him, and they sat in a coffee house watching the rain through the window while he talked about the people he had met, the new ideas he had to make money and the brilliant opportunities offered by Berlin.

"So much more is happening here than back home. This is a city of great careers. I am going to write a book with this title. Berlin, city of careers."

Her German was elementary. Her head was spinning trying to make sense out of what she saw outside. People rushed by under tightly gripped umbrellas. Beggars, crippled in the last war, leaned against a wall under the shelter of shutters. Glittering shop windows were packed with unfamiliar goods and unreadable signs.

His face was animated now as he ordered another round of coffee, this time with a brioche they selected from a trolley. But his body, the body she knew so well, was skeletal now. She had to feed him up.

They stepped out into the rain at seven o'clock to get to the antique shop after closing time. He fumbled with the keys at the door, and she had time to look up at the grey sky, a narrow strip of clouds, so much narrower in this narrow street than the sky back home on Podmaniczky Street.

7

Almost Riefenstahl

There is no childhood photo of my mother to be found. As if she didn't exist before she met my father. After that, there are a lot of them.

Sitting on a rock wall by Lake Balaton on a cloudy day. Walking triumphantly down a path in the short skirt of a '20s flapper, showing off her perfect legs.

Father often said that they were the most beautiful in Budapest and should be insured for a million dollars like the legs of Marlene Dietrich.

And there is the snapshot taken of them by a stranger at a soccer match with the bustling stadium behind them, a couple so young, so together, so happy. Both of them are slim and brimming with energy. The angle is from below highlighting their tall figures stepping in unison, looking ahead.

Almost Riefenstahl.

That's a shocking thing to say. But it is not anachronistic. They were of the same generation as Leni, Hitler's fetching panegyrist. They breathed the same Berlin air. And it was Leni's cinematographic innovation to photograph marching feet from a low angle that made them look potent and to capture the heads proudly held high, looking ahead to the promise of a triumphant future.

8

Father's choices

It took seven years for my parents to get married. Only much later did I understand the difficulties they faced.

As a child, I looked at them as if they started to exist on the day I was born. In my eyes, they had no previous life and no other function than to look after me as my preordained father (Apu) and mother (Anyu).

How could I know that forming a family needed courage at that time?

Apu's devotion to a Roman Catholic girl of peasant stock was not welcomed by his relations. For him, choosing Anyu was not only a choice of love; it was also an assertion of his independence.

Anyu's family was equally set against her choosing a Jew, and even worse, a "bohemian journalist" without reliable income at a time when the Great Depression was still in full bloom, when unemployed professionals stood in line for soup and shovelled snow for a crust.

After my arrival, the vocal objections seemed to die away and were replaced by mute disapproval.

I was delivered by the leading Budapest gynaecologist, József Frigyesi, in his clinic. That set a pattern. Throughout my childhood Apu insisted that even with trivial problems I had to see the best specialists he managed to find.

Anyu said it was an easy birth.

She was smiling on the photo taken by Apu's Rolleiflex, her hair still in wet disarray on a pillow next to her newborn.

My first home was a rented room in a tenement house on the Pest side, and I was still breastfed when my mother found her first job after Berlin. Apu's income having become more and more unreliable, it was Anyu's pay that kept us going.

She had to call upon her Roman Catholic mother to look after me. I was christened in Grandma's faith and raised by her to become a devout girl according to the tenets of her religion.

Between Two Wars

As an only child, I was surrounded by the undivided love and attention of my parents. But it was Grandma who spent every day with me, whose view of the world and whose reactions to the smallest details of my expanding universe defined my early years and left an enduring benchmark for the rest of my life.

9

A whiff of ammonia

Grandma wears cotton aprons, dark, but faded in endless washings, sprinkled with a pattern of small white flowers. I can smell the apron, vaguely scented by onions and garlic, by the ashes she's emptied from the potbelly stove and maybe a whiff of ammonia, if she has been scrubbing the kitchen floor.

I like to lay my head in her lap, my cheek resting on her apron, and feel her fingers on my scalp as they search among locks of hair.

She is a great lice catcher.

*

It is only now that I am attempting to put together bits and pieces of her life and to ask why she was such a strong-minded woman.

As the firstborn in her family, Grandma had to assume the role of a mother while she was still a child. Born in 1882, she was followed a year later by baby Zsófia. Then came a boy, János, then two more brothers, including my favourite, Uncle Pista, in 1888 when she was six years old.

It was in Uncle Pista's one room adobe house where I, a scrawny great niece of his from Budapest, spent my unforgettable summer holidays.

Grandma was 12 when another brother arrived and was christened Géza. He was destined to die as a soldier in the First World War when he was in his early 20s (nobody knows exactly when) in faraway Galicia.

Géza was followed by two baby sisters: Juliska and Ilona.

Ilona, Grandma's last sister, was born three years after Grandma gave birth to my mother. Grandma got pregnant when she was 19.

This was the way generations mingled and rolled on.

Because her parents were poor landless peasants, they both had to work for wages in the fields, getting up at sunrise, getting back after sunset. It was left to Grandma to look after her siblings. She fed them, cooked, washed, bathed them, dressed them, learned to mend and sew. She knew how to rock them to sleep, how to calm them with the songs she later taught me, when I needed to be calmed. She knew how to cut their hair, their nails, how to console them when they cried and how to discipline them when they quarreled with each other.

Then she did all this for her own three children, two of whom reached adulthood, while one died still an infant, a boy whose grave

I often visited with her.

By the time I came along, she had seen much and understood more than most books could teach.

I arrived when she was 51 years old and soon to become a widow.

10

Born by the Danube

Grandma's maiden name was Markó Etel. Püski, her birthplace, was a small village beside the Danube, not far from the Austrian border in a picturesque area called *Kisalföld* (small lowland) dominated by the river.

The Danube nurtured there the rich soil through time immemorial. The molten snow of the Alps and the Carpathian mountains poured into the lowlands flooding villages and creating shifting gravel mounds alongside new islands. It was a mercurial land of fishermen, gold prospectors, rebels and day labourers, mud hut builders, dreamers and fugitives from wars or laws. Bishops and aristocrats owned most of the cultivable parts for centuries.

No matter how smart Grandma appeared to be, she had to quit school as soon as she learned to read and write. As she grew strong enough to go to work on the fields, she left the young ones to her sister and became a labourer. She excelled with the sickle and could handle the scythe as well, a rare aptitude among young girls.

She already had an illegitimate child, my mother, when she married a coachman in Budapest. She was still beautiful, and he was happy to adopt the child.

I called that coachman Grandpa. The only grandpa I knew.

To keep poverty at bay, she bought an old Singer and started to sew and mend, mostly patching elbows and replacing workingmen's shirt collars that always wore out first around the neck. I watched her cut the still unblemished shirttail to make a matching new collar out of the material, replacing the missing tail with a scrap of cotton that didn't need to match because it wasn't visible tucked inside pants.

I can still see her. An old woman bending over to thread the needle. Her wire-rimmed glasses sit on the end of her nose, her tongue is stuck out resting on her lower lip, a sign of concentration my mother inherited and so did I. I see her fumble and sigh, then straighten up, roll the wheel with her right hand, her feet starting to pump the foot pedal, while her left hand feeds the cloth under the jumping needle. I can hear the old Singer rattling its tune, the comforting melody of my childhood.

11

The sweet smell of wool slippers

When I was two, my parents moved into a three-storey house of eight apartments on Lehel Street and rented a one-room flat equipped with all the modern comforts. The building also housed the ground floor offices of a large factory dedicated to making sweet-smelling felt slippers.

Their choice may have been influenced by the relatively low rent owing to the noise and pollution associated with the attached factory, although that didn't alleviate their monthly anxiety when the rent was due.

This house became the setting I explored from age two to 12. It was my first school, teaching me about people, secrets, work and war.

Our place was on the first floor. A door with a glass inlay led into an entry hall big enough to take three steps inside in every direction. Four white doors opened from this hall taking up all the wall space.

The one on the right led into the kitchen which was big enough to take seven steps in any direction and which housed a gas stove, a sideboard, a faucet with a sink and a table with two *hokedli*s serving as seats. Their drawers contained such things as shoe polish brushes and kitchen rags. The window was next to the tap. In the summer it was open all the time so that flies, the smells of cooking from other kitchens and the odour of raw wool bales from the factory yard could float in.

The second door led to a pantry big enough to take two steps in all directions. It was lined with shelves where Grandma kept jars of jams and bottles of tomato paste. On the floor were boxes for onions and potatoes. The tiny window of the pantry opened into a dark airshaft shared with the window of the toilet and the bathroom.

The third door led to our toilet, big enough to sit down or to stand when I pulled down my pants. A wood handle hung on a chain overhead. It had to be pulled to flush the water from a box attached to the wall above. A small window was set high left of the seat.

The fourth door led into a room with a big window looking into the yard. One could take twelve big steps here in all directions if one could remove all the furniture. In one corner was the double bed for Apu and Anyu. Behind the door was my *sezlony,* a couch by day when my bedding was stuffed under the mattress of the big bed. Another wall was taken up by a wardrobe. Next to the window was Apu's desk with his bronze lion standing on a marble inkwell, and in the middle of the room stood the dining table with four chairs. In winter the potbelly stove was pulled away from the wall and the table was pushed closer to the window to make room for the coal fire.

Behind my *sezlony* was the bathroom door leading into a six-step-long narrow space with a window opening into the airshaft it shared with the toilet and the pantry. This window played an important part in the last months of the war as an escape route for Apu, when I came running to warn him about approaching danger.

How fast I could run! Only my heart ran faster than my feet up the stairs. I'd burst through the door, but never shout. Only whisper.

12

Tunnel terror

Could it be that we are born with built-in risk receptors? That we find things to be afraid of from the moment we draw our first breath? We don't need to read horror stories or watch ghouls haunting derelict castles on the screen, our fears start before we can focus our eyes, before we can read. To this day, I shudder at a sudden noise behind my back and avoid the edges of things.

As I grew from infant to toddler with my world widening from cot to room, to house, to street, my phobias kept up with my progress.

One of the places I dreaded was the *alagút*, a tunnel two blocks from our house that we called the *tunel*. The first time I laid eyes on it, Grandma led me by the hand down Bulcsú Street.

We descended from the sidewalk on what seemed to be a steep slope and briskly stepped over percussive steel plates at the entrance. As we entered a vault of darkness, leaving behind us the blinding sunlight, a sudden coolness enveloped us. The scent of damp walls, a sweating ceiling, mould and piss was overwhelming. It was like entering a dark underworld, a cavity of echoing footsteps that were spasmodically interrupted by a terrifying roar and screech of steel-upon-steel whenever a train passed overhead heading for the Nyugati Railroad Station. The few dim light bulbs installed to combat the darkness had no chance against a single sharp beam from far away. This pinpoint of brightness held out the promise of an exit.

I gripped Grandma's hand tightly and, instead of looking at my feet, I stared at the silhouettes of backlit bodies coming towards us, floating ghosts in the distance at first, slowly growing in menace.

As the years passed, the *tunel* did not lose its menace despite my maturing mind coming to understand the need for a prosaic crossing under the railway lines. Gradually, I learned to discriminate among the passers-by, to recognize the unsteady drunks who urinated against the walls, the tired women lugging baskets of produce from the Lehel Street market towards their flats in the 6th District, boys with their school satchels slung over their shoulders skipping to avoid stepping on cracks and young mothers dragging toddlers the way I was dragged by Grandma on the day of my initiation.

As my steps became longer and quicker I would try to get ahead of Grandma, showing off my independence, knowing that she was behind me, ready to protect me.

When we emerged from the *tunel,* we were only a couple of blocks from the house where Grandma lived on Podmaniczky Street. It was a big house, taller than our building, with circular gangways leading to the flats on four floors stacked above each other.

It seemed far away when she first took me there. We wound our way up the staircase to the third floor, and Grandma opened a door at the end of the narrow corridor. I had to learn the name of her formidable landlady, Aunt Matild, and to say *kistihand* when I bobbed with a curtsy in front of her. She was a big woman in a stiffly starched apron, her shirtsleeves rolled up above her elbows that she kept spread wide like a hen taking a dust bath. It was hard to get by her in the small kitchen. She usually handed me an apple she wiped on her belly to make it shine.

Grandma asked me sit down on her bed. I gathered that it made her feel proud that it was right next to the window. "I don't share it with anybody," she said. There were three other beds in the room crammed against the walls. One belonged to Aunt Matild, the other two to four men who were cleaners at the railroad station. "They work on different shifts, so they can use the same beds in turn," Grandma said quietly not to wake the present occupants.

The apples of Aunt Matild were ripe and sweet, but embarrassingly noisy. I was careful not to bite the small pink worms I used to find near the core. I used to take them home. They were easy to collect in a glass jar with small holes in the lid to allow fresh air.

I grew fond of watching them crawl along the leaves I dropped in the jar for their bedding. Grandma told me to feed them apple bits. They didn't get along well with caterpillars and the bigger worms I found on the hairy tips of corncobs.

Then one day I was with Grandma up in the attic helping her hang out the laundry. Suddenly I noticed a pile of pigeon feathers under a beam. They were fluttering. I bent down close and I saw under the feathers the bird's body riddled with squirming maggots.

"Fly-blown," said Grandma.

"So many," I whispered.

"Maggots. They will tidy it up," she said. "They will leave only the bones and the feathers."

"Terrible."

"What's terrible? It's the order of nature. What do you think will eat us when we die?"

I ran down the stairs, grabbed my glass jar and flushed my worm collection down the WC. By then, I was not afraid of the *tunel.* The time was ripe for another kind of menace.

13

How to pull a tooth

Grandma wraps me in a big towel after my bath. Only my toes are sticking out. She dries them with the corner of the towel before she grabs hold of my big toe.

I laugh. I know the chant that is about to start.

Ez elment vadászni.

Ez meglőtte.
Ez hazavitte.
Ez megsütötte.
Ez az ici-pici mind megette.

Such a simple game. Grabbing the big toe, then grabbing one by one each of the other four, ending up with the little toe, assigning a task to each. The game ends with a tickle across my sole, an irresistible tickle that sends me into a storm of giggles.

The big toe has gone a-hunting.
This one shot it.
This took it home.
This baked it.
And this itsy-bitsy ate it all.

What gets shot and what the little toe eats I never learn.

Anyu and Apu have no time to play these games. They are off on their breadwinning routes, Anyu in offices 48 or more hours a week, Apu chasing after stories, searching for chances to earn a few *pengős.*

Grandma is there when I wake up. She is there when I go to sleep. She is the one who teaches me the songs and tricks of childhood. How to paint Easter eggs, how to make my doll a bed sticking prickly thistles together.

Egy, megérett a meggy
Kettő, feneketlen teknő
Három, te vagy az én párom
Négy, hová mégy
Öt, fejed a tök
Hat, hasad a pad

and so on…

All the numbers line up with immediate images:

one, ripe sour cherry
two, a bottomless tub
three, you and me make a pair
four, where are you going?
five, your head is a pumpkin
six, your belly a bench
and so on… (It is almost impossible to translate the snappy Hungarian rhymes…)

I learn the numbers by hopping along, reciting the rhyming ditties while trying to keep up with Grandma's longer legs on the way to the market.

14

Grandma's mouth

She had a voice that was half a hum and half the faltering remnant of a once lilting soprano spoiled by a lisp. The distinctive sound of her chants was due to the way her relaxed tongue produced an unmistakable *Szigetköz* twang. Her missing teeth caused her softened consonants She had only one incisor left, and even this one was loose, hanging down in the front of her maxilla. Her other teeth had been lost along the way during a lifetime of tight circumstances.

Who needed a dentist to pull a tooth? If it hurts, she said, it is a cinch to get rid of it. You wind a string around the culprit and tie the end of the string to a door handle. By suddenly jerking the door open, the tooth is forced to fly out in a blinding flash.

I was worried about the possibility of her demonstrating this with my teeth. I didn't want to be toothless.

She was once a legendary beauty, as some old men in Püski remembered her long after her death. Her beauty survived in her smile (lips closed, blue eyes locked into my eyes denoting undivided attention), which she doled out to me generously through my first 17 years, until the day she died of a heart attack sitting by the fireplace and railing against the deceptively benign constitution of the Soviet Union.

"A bunch of lies," she said.

15

A waiting room for heaven

Grandma took on the task of teaching me religion, seeing that Apu and Anyu didn't bother. She did this mostly in the kitchen while she was peeling potatoes or stirring a stew.

"Do you want to go to heaven?"

I had heard about heaven before. People sometimes said, "He went to heaven." Or called a Sunday stroll under the acacias "almost like heaven". Or said "heavenly" when they bit into a chocolate bonbon.

So I said, "Yes," with some eagerness.

"It's not that easy. Not everybody gets there."

"Why? Where do they go?"

"They go to hell."

I knew about hell. I heard people say, "Go to hell", and they were always angry when they said it. It had to be a bad place.

"Sometimes they can go to purgatory, if they are not that bad," said Grandma.

"Where is that?"

"It's like a waiting room for heaven."

"Like at the doctor's place," I said.

"Not quite. It hurts. You have to suffer there. To pay for your sins for a time."

"Heaven is best," I decided.

"You must deserve heaven. Must work at it."

"What can I do?"

"You must pray every day."

"Is it difficult?"

"Of course, not." She lowered herself on a *hokedli* and motioned me to sit on her lap.

I climbed up. I was ready.

"First you have to put your hands together like this. Flat. Thumb on thumb. Straighten your fingers. Good."

I sat with my hands held stiffly against my chest. It wasn't too bad. My feet were dangling in the air, and I was swinging them as usual. Grandma put her hands on my feet and said, "Stop it. This is not a game. When you pray, you must concentrate on every word and must be sincere."

"Sincere?"

"You must mean every word. Each and every one must come from your heart."

"My heart?"

"Yes, it must. Otherwise it doesn't count. You need to think of God and talk to him personally."

"Where is he?"

"In heaven, of course. And if you want to get there and meet him, you must show that you love him. Then he will love you."

"So I can't play when I talk to him."

"No, the best thing is to kneel."

"Where?"

"I'll teach you an evening prayer to say before you go to bed in the evening. You kneel by your bed. Put your elbows on the mattress, raise your eyes towards heaven and say this little prayer."

"And he will love me..."

"He will smile down upon you."

"Will I see him?"

"No, he remains invisible."

It took me no time to learn the prayer. It started with, "My sweet God, my spirit whispers thanks for your daily succour." And it ended with "I repent my many sins. May the blood of your Holy Son rinse my heart pure white."

Every night when she was the one who put me to bed, Grandma turned down my *dunyha*, and I knelt down by my pillow to thank God and ask him to forgive and love me.

I never saw Apu and Anyu pray, and Grandma encouraged me to pray for them. When she taught me the *Pater Noster* and the *Hail Mary*, she proposed that I offer those to God and beg Him to care for them even if they neglected Him. For a long while, I followed her advice in the hope of securing a place for them in the waiting room of Heaven.

16

Bedbugs

I am helping Grandma to find bedbugs hiding behind pictures hanging on the wall under the curled-up paper on the back of the frames. She shows me how to skewer them with an open safety pin.

"Look," she proudly holds up the lethal pinhead to display a fat one bloated with blood. "This one's not going to get you tonight."

The hunt for bedbugs is exciting. She says it's a hopeless effort because the house is old. "They like it here. They know every crack and crevice in every apartment. They can climb up and down alongside plumbing pipes and electric wires into every room. When we smoke them out of one room, they flee up or down or sideways, ready to move back when the smoke is gone."

I don't mind hunting them, but I hate the sulphuric smoke of fumigation. It is better to take off the pictures from the wall, skewer the beasts and wipe the frames with kerosene to keep them away.

"They don't like the smell," Grandma says.

Next year we do it again.

The same is true of cockroaches. They nest in the coal cellar and scavenge up and down the house every night. When I switch on the light in the kitchen, they run for cover in the cracks along the walls.

They are a part of our lives, a part we don't brag about.

17

Szabolcs, Lehel and Bulcsu

Our address was Lehel Street 4/B.

The house is still standing, although it is totally changed. They added two more storeys on the top after 1956 and reduced the stairwell by the addition of an elevator.

Before the war, Lehel Street was lined by rows of tall acacias blooming in the spring and shading the sidewalks in summer. It was alive with traffic and with pedestrians in and out of shops and pubs.

I loved to watch pigeons preening on the acacia branches. Sometimes one of their droppings landed on my shoulder. I was told that it was a drop of good luck.

We had bright yellow streetcars (Number 90) that clattered down the rails and came to a squealing halt on the corner. The uniformed ticket seller held his leather satchel tightly against his side as he leaned out and pulled a strap to ring a bell telling the driver when he could move on because everybody had disembarked or boarded safely. Then the long jangling train took off towards Berliner Square.

Szabolcs Street was different. Although it was also named after a legendary chief like our Lehel, it had no streetcars. No automobiles seemed to stop there, nor big trucks or horse-drawn carriages loaded with barrels of beer trundled over its cobblestones. To me it seemed dead, leading nowhere.

We were taught at school about Szabolcs and Lehel, commanders of thousands of Magyar fighters who ranged westward, pillaging towns and villages for almost a whole century. They used successful hit-and-run tactics against the scattered fiefs. We were told that both of them were hanged in August 955, after the battle of Augsburg which they lost to Otto I, the Great.

According to a legend, disproved by historians today, but still believed in Hungary by adherents to patriotic legends, Otto granted Lehel his last wish, allowing him to blow his famous horn. When he was handed the carved ivory instrument, he stepped forward and smote the king on his head with such force that he died instantly. Then Lehel declared: "You go ahead first to be my servant in the next world." It was supposedly the belief of Magyars that whomever they killed would be their servant in an afterlife.

Soon after his victory, Otto, still very much alive, was promoted by Pope John XII to become a Holy Roman Emperor, not a bad title for a man condemned to eternal servitude by Lehel.

That defeat spelled the end of the old "Hungarian Century" when our cavalry of more than 40,000 men galloped through what today are Germany, Italy, Switzerland and France, raiding as far as Spain.

We, the children growing up on Lehel Street, were inordinately proud of Lehel, having learned that the Christians of those lands in the west included in their prayers the entreaty: "Lord, deliver us from the arrows of the Magyars."

Szabolcs didn't have a magic horn chipped by the head of a king, and his street appeared lacking in distinction to me.

Until our family historian, Terike, who died in 2009, in that year sent me a note on a scrap of paper that I still keep:

"Dear Panni, you were born in the Frigyesi Klinika, Szabolcs Street 33-35. I don't remember which district it was in 1933. They've redrawn districts so many times."

So a Szabolcs Street clinic was my birthplace. That is where the famous clinic was located.

Why did I think that it was only a street of tenements with long corridors and communal WCs tucked next to the stairwell on every floor?

The street that Grandma and I took towards the *tunel* was also named after a great warrior mate of Lehel called Bulcsu. It was Bulcsu's job to connect Lehel and Szabolcs Streets.

I grew up surrounded by these historic names up to age 12 when we left Lehel Street 4/B for Kárpát Street 7/B, and moved to the third floor into Apartment 12/A. It should have been Apartment 13, but that number was widely believed to bring bad luck and was hardly ever used.

Come to think of it, *Kárpát* means Carpathian, the name of the mountain chain embracing what before the First World War used to be Hungarian territory, a chain whose high, snow-capped peaks with their dangerous passes are also steeped in history.

Our teachers were most eloquent when they described the battles fought through the ages on what seemed to us every square inch of the Carpathian Basin.

A child watching

Death knocks
in corridors
and may appear
at odd hours
uninvited.

Death has his whims,
may skip a door
choose another
in the crowded
apartment house.

He plays grim games
with families
and may come back
until no one
is left to grab.

then may remain
in a bare flat
which is re-let
to another
unfortunate

who knows nothing
of the secret
wily flatmate
lying in wait
with a bent blade.

18

Tidy girls are pretty

The tidy girl song is very old. I am sure. Grandma told me that she learned it when she was a child.

In Hungarian:

Zöld erdőben jártam
virágok között
ott láttam egy kislányt
bokrétát kötött

mondtam neki hogy
maga aranyos
akkor szép a kislány
mikor takaros.

Roughly translated it goes like this:

I strolled in a forest
and among flowers
spotted a young lass.
I said to her that
you are made of gold
a girl neat and tidy
lovely to behold.

I learned to sing it before I could read and write. I thought it was about me. I sang it for years wanting to be tidy, wanting to be pretty, wanting to be noticed when I was picking flowers. This song taught me what it was to be a girl, a sweet girl, a proper girl seeking approval.

To be a girl spied upon by hidden eyes in the forest was also thrilling.

I can hear Grandma's voice now.

Her uneven breath made her pause at the wrong places as she sang. I knew that her heart was not right (they called it by a long name: coronary thrombosis). She still tried to lift me when I was already old enough to go to school, but she ran out of breath when she tried to keep up with me rushing ahead of her on the street.

19

The scent of pines

The week before Christmas a pine forest invaded the bare ground behind Lehel Market. The trees came and conquered the lot that stretched towards the massive church of The Blessed Árpadházi Margit. Freshly cut and of all sizes - ranging from knee-high up to more than two meters – they lined up on the icy snow among the steaming horses and peasant carts that hauled them to the city.

Grandma asked me to help her select the right tree, but when I would point at one, she would shake her head and let the snowflakes trapped on her forehead trickle down her nose.

I followed her from tree to tree and listened to her haggle with shuffling, coughing men who laughed and made dismissive gestures with their hands. They wore knitted wool mittens similar to mine. One of them had on gloves without fingers, and he kept his hands warm by blowing puffs of his breath on his nails and sticking them under his armpits.

The frost pinched my nose and got hold of my feet. My hands in my pockets and my ears tucked into my wool cap remained sensible, but my toes had grown numb. I looked at the horses and stopped to watch two of them standing with their heads hanging, their manes thick with snow. Next to them, an old woman stood bundled in a black wool scarf that made her look like a giant black ball sprinkled with powdered sugar. She performed a sort of dance by stomping her boots on the ice. I tried to imitate her doing a slow tap dance myself, but my feet refused to obey. All I could do was rub my ankles together and think about a hot mug of *kakaó*.

We circled among the rows of pine and clusters of women shoppers who seemed to make up their mind much faster than Grandma.

On the way home, I carried the top end of the chosen tree while Grandma hugged the heavier bottom. It was a triumphal march enhanced by the fresh scent of pine. The large bottom branches swept the sidewalk until I held my end higher, trying to lift my arms like a priest proudly raising the Host towards heaven. My feet forgot to hurt, and my eyes stayed glued on Grandma's bobbing back.

We filled a bucket with soil and pebbles pushing the pine trunk all the way down to the bottom, so that the tree stood up straight. Then we cleared a space under the window and carried the tree inside. If the top leaned one way or another, we could always find a string and tie a branch to the window handle to straighten it.

It was left up to the angels on Christmas Eve to bring the decorations, drape the pine with silver strands, cover it with angel hair and to light the dozens of candles and "star-throwers" that would light up the room with magic.

I never had a chance to see the angels. I had to hide in the bathroom and wait to be called. Anyu and Apu were allowed to meet them while I buried my face into Anyu's quilted robe hanging on the door and tried to decipher the whispers and flutters that I was happy to attribute to the flapping of angelic wings.

When finally the bathroom door opened, I could step out and see the glowing, sparkling tree. The guttering candles reacted to every breath and every movement as they played with their own reflections in the tinsel-wrapped sweet fondants hanging on every branch. The breathtaking spectacle always made me stop and stare. For a moment I'd forget about finding my presents.

It may have been 1936 or '37 when I saw my first crying doll under the tree. It was lying in its own four-wheeled pram. It was the most beautiful porcelain doll I've ever seen. It had curly brown hair and identical brown eyelashes. When I lifted her up, she opened her blue eyes. When I put her down, she whimpered like a kitten. She had porcelain arms and legs, and her trunk was stuffed with sawdust. She had a pink dress on and white socks with black patent leather shoes. There are some rare moments in life suffused by a sense of total contentment. Lifting her out of the pram was such a moment. Laying her down again, watching her eyes close and hearing her cry was another. I did it over and over again. Luckily, I didn't drop her. Never.

20

Zigzag memories

When I write, memories never come in a straight line. They hurtle at me in a staggering disarray. I remember clearly and in almost tactile detail happy days, but moments of pain are cut short, although more acute.

Could it be that it is in my nature to select tenderness and delight and avoid dealing with the shocks?

When I can describe the eyes of a porcelain doll in loving detail, why don't I want to describe a rearing horse in the factory yard that impaled with the carriage shaft a driver who was trying to calm it? Why did I try to forget?

When I heard the groan of that driver and saw him crumple and die under the weight of a hoof landing on his back, why did I turn away? Why did I go inside trying to avoid seeing the details of his removal and witnessing the prolonged beating of the horse that I could hear clearly inside?

Where is the balance?

Getting the true measure of life?

Am I a reliable teller of my story?

Or am I sugar-coating?

Can I trust myself?

I am 60 percent water

It flows in my veins
rinces my brains
drenches my muscles
and softens my heart.

It makes me part
of the Pacific
the salty mix
of all the oceans.

I contain
the monsoon rains
of Bangladesh
and the icebergs
calfing off Antarctica.

I am one with the Amazon
the waters of
the Rhine and the Rhone
and I drank the Danube
fed by the snow
that fell on the Alps
and the Carpathians.

My body carries
the clouds racing
over Hiroshima
and emptying
into the Thames
lapping London
where I drank them
piping hot
sipping gingerly
as my morning tea.

21

The cobbler's shop

When the shoes I had to wear on Sundays to museums, coffee houses or other important occasions started to wear out, it meant an impending visit to the local cobbler's shop.

First came a cleansing ceremony. I watched Grandma unfold and spread an old *Pesti Hirlap* on a stool, take out the boxes of shoe polish from a drawer together with rags, old toothbrushes and a knife for scraping off mud or dry horse manure. I was allowed to open the boxes of polish (black, brown and colourless) that had small handles twirling on a spindle. The lids lifted obediently, and I placed the open boxes on the newspaper.

Grandma would polish and brush and buff to make them shine before we took them to the cobbler's. That was a matter of pride and respect. Self-respect and respect for the tradesman.

We stuffed the down-at-heel shoes into her wicker basket and walked around the corner to Bulcsu Street where I could glimpse the latest DKW and BMW automobiles. We carried on past Tüzér Street with its grey buildings to the next corner to reach the shop.

I'd let go of Grandma's hand as soon as we stepped on the sidewalk and could glimpse the dusty cotton curtains behind the small windows sunk below the sidewalk. The cobbler lived in a cellar under a sign depicting a black boot and saying *Cipész*. I still remember his name because Apu used it for years whenever he needed one for an amusing character in a satire.

We descended on stone steps, and I noticed that Grandma never knocked. We just entered and, if we didn't see a soul at the counter, Grandma would holler, "Good day, Mr Czibulka!"

Why did she raise her voice? The cellar was a single room, and Czibulka was always close, even if momentarily invisible behind makeshift curtains hanging on ropes that crisscrossed his shop delineating the various activities of his family.

Behind what seemed like an old sheet hung up to dry, slept his four children. I guessed that they were two boys and two girls, but it was hard to be sure with each of them having the same length of hair and the same freckled face peering at us from the shelter of a sheet. Behind what looked like a red-checkered tablecloth was Mrs Czibulka, a formidable woman of wide girth standing by a stove stirring something. Mr Czibulka hurried to the counter, where Grandma tried to put our basket, pushing aside piles of old shoes to make room.

The cobbler, who was much shorter than Grandma, had big hands and thick, ropy arms, bare under his rolled up shirtsleeves. He lifted each of my shoes separately. He held them close to his chin and turned them around, rubbing them with his fingers that stopped to investigate each crack and hole, stroking them as if they were injured animals. When he put them down, he looked up above his glasses and inquired about Grandma's health.

"No complaints at the moment," she would say. She never complained about her legs; only told me and no one else when they started to swell. "And how are your children doing?"

"Juli is coughing less. But Nusi's eczema is spreading to her neck."

"I have heard of a cream," Grandma said. "I'll inquire further."

"Wednesday morning?" Czibulka asked.

"Could you do them by Monday? That's the only pair that fits Panni."

"Monday evening," Czibulka said.

"Thank you. I might have something for Nusi by Monday," Grandma grabbed the empty basket, ready to leave.

The children followed her every move from under the sheet. Four pairs of bare feet dangled off their mattress.

When we were back on the street, Grandma took my hand and sighed. I think she said the same thing every time we went there: "Poor Mr Czibulka. Four fragile children and a deaf-mute wife. Life is hard."

As she speeded up sunk in her thoughts, I had to run to keep up with her. I imagined what it would be like to be a Czibulka child, giggling and wrestling on a mattress. Living in a cellar where everything happened behind sheets, among mountains of shoes in need of mending by a father who was always there. And having a silent mother who didn't go to work but cooked all the time. Living where people entered without the formality of knocking on the door. It could be fun to have brothers and sisters.

"I might have something for Nusi," Grandma said. "But nobody can help Juli. She has tuberculosis. She won't live long. It's a pity that they are crammed in that small space. She might pass it on to the others."

When we got home, I didn't settle inside. I brought out a *sámli* from the kitchen and sat down in the sun beside a tub of oleanders. I suddenly felt lucky to live where I lived in our neat little flat filled with books and pillows, with Apu's shiny brass lion sitting on his inkwell. To live with dark veneered furniture, with a kitchen and a bathroom with doors that could be closed, with a dining table holding a vase full of lilacs. I was glad that Anyu and Apu went away to work and left Grandma and me alone all day with nobody bringing us old shoes.

22

The feel of new shoes

Buying a pair of new shoes involved a ritual almost as elaborate as an incense-soaked 10 o'clock mass in our Church of Árpádházi Boldog Margit.

Just entering the shoe shop with its tinkling bell over the door announcing our arrival made me feel like an important actor stepping up on stage. The smell of the paper boxes lining the walls floor to ceiling mingled with the stronger aroma of leather made every intake of breath out of the ordinary.

The salesman, elderly and gaunt, the same one always in attendance, guided us with elaborate welcoming gestures to chairs set up in a row under a chandelier suspended from the high ceiling. As I climbed up on the seat assigned to me, Anyu would tell the attentively leaning gentleman what she wanted and he would answer sotto voce with his head nodding in sympathy.

"Her feet are growing so fast," she'd complain with a tinge of pride.

"Of course, of course," he agreed before disappearing behind a door to reappear with a towering stack of boxes.

"Take off your shoes and straighten your socks for Mr Kovács," Anyu ordered.

When he opened all the boxes and arranged them in a circular display around Anyu, he'd kneel down in front of me, making me feel as the Páduai Szent Antal statue in church. I often knelt there alongside Grandma, who would prompt me to pray and ask the clever saint to help us find something we'd lost. A glove. Some money. Keys.

The most important part of the ritual was my role of walking around on the carpeted floor while Anyu and Mr Kovács watched every step I took between the chairs and a mirror.

"How does it feel?" Anyu asked every time. They always felt harder and heavier than my old pair.

"A bit big," I'd say, feeling my feet sliding around inside.

Mr Kovács, still kneeling when I sat down again, would press on the top of a shoe looking for the end of my big toe. He'd offer a smile and point to the empty space there.

"She'll grow into it in no time," Anyu said to him without consulting me.

By alternating between oversized shoes and outgrown shoes, we managed to make each pair last long with several visits in between to the Czibulkas for new heels or soles. And when even repairs could not help any more, the old ones achieved additional longevity by a hole cut in front for the comfort of my ungainly big toes. They would still do for hopscotch in the dust of the factory yard.

23

Church magic

On Sunday mornings the courtyard is abandoned. The machines fall silent in the factory. The lights are turned off in the offices on the ground floor.

For Grandma there is no rest. I have to be made ready for church. I can't be late. Now that I am a student of the Aréna Avenue School, it is my duty as a Roman Catholic to be on time. I have to be there before the basket disappears. A piece of paper with my name legibly written on it has to be in the wicker basket by the sacristy door to be stamped when the mass starts and to be returned to the door and picked up at the end. An immaculate attendance record is necessary for my first communion.

Grandma is busy ironing a fresh skirt for me and making breakfast even before Anyu and Apu open their eyes. They look like a big single lump under the covers.

I throw back my warm *dunyha,* sit up and shiver on the edge of the *sezlony*, half-awake, but happy. I love dressing for church. The fact that the whole congregation wear their best shoes, finest coats and hats, fine silk stockings with runs repaired and gloves as well, makes churchgoing an occasion of pride and spectacle.

The organ music, the trembling candles and the statues of gold-robed saints studding the walls enhance the grandeur of the embroidered garments of the priest and the glow of the colorful stained glass windows. The Lehel Street church is our Sunday theatre. The altar is bedecked with bouquets of fresh flowers. The altar boys shake hand-held bells at precise intervals and release puffs of incense that make me dizzy. I am part of the crowd of extras singing in unison, standing and kneeling, making the sign of the cross on our forehead, shoulders and chest. I love the *mea culpas,* having learned to thump my heart with my right fist while I repeat them and imagine the vivid, terrible sins I might commit one day.

24

Chin-chin, hen-in-pants

First grade started at age six, but I couldn't enter until I was almost seven because the cut-off date started on September first, and I was born at the end of October. So I was a big, almost-seven-year-old girl by the time I enrolled at the Aréna Avenue School.

A beautiful school, I thought. It was on a corner of Lehel Street and the avenue, a short walking distance from our place. It had two entrances, one for boys and one for girls. We didn't see the boys, who only existed after school on the street, gathered in bunches ready to strike. They not only shouted stupid things when we went by, but also ran after us to pull our hair. We didn't know their names, so we tagged them according to their looks: Fatty, Shorty, Big Ears, Pimply, Curly, Dummy. It took me less than a year not to be afraid of them. When we spotted them hiding in a doorway, we just ran and laughed. We were fast.

Our first teacher of religion was a nun of improbable height. When she came through the classroom door for the first time, we held our breath fearing that she would hit the top of the doorframe. She reminded us of a vertical ironing board in her ankle-length robe, tight on her body, dark blue, almost black. It buttoned up high on her neck, and she wore on her head a sort of kerchief of the same colour.

I don't remember her name. She could have been Sister Cecilia or Sister Bernadette, maybe Esperanza, most likely a strange name of at least three syllables. She was soft-spoken and gentle and didn't hit us with a ruler. She punished with silence. If one of us was called upon to recite our *katekizmus* lesson and failed to remember a word, she stood there silently staring at the culprit for what seemed to us an eternity.

Once it happened to me. I used *sacrilegious* instead of *blasphemous* and knew it the moment I said it. She stared at me and folded her arms, waiting. I started stuttering and gulping for air wanting to sink down into the floor, then on to the floor below and through the layer of linoleum covering the gym all the way to the fiery furnace in the center of the Earth, which I believed was the proper Hell furnished with brimstones and lava.

She stood motionless. My brain was boiling. After a while she said,

"You may stand until you remember." She said it very kindly, not as an order, but a request. Then she walked away from me, stepped up on the *katedra* and started talking about the immaculate conception. About the angel appearing in front of the astonished Virgin Mary.

The moment she described the angel flying away through the window, I remembered and loudly shouted the right word: "*Blasphemous!*"

She froze. There was a long silence. Then she said, "Go and sit in the last row." That was the first time I had to sit in the seat of shame.

She was kind. She could have sent me to the principal, or could have made me stand outside in the corridor until the bell rang. That was a dangerous place because, if the principal walked by, he would ask why I was there, and it could have had serious consequences. Sitting in the last row was a much milder punishment, even better than standing or kneeling in the corner of the room with my back to the class.

After that incident, I started to dream about her. She came to me floating in the air with a broom between her legs, her habit billowing and flapping behind her like bat's wings. Her black stockings and black shoes, usually hidden under her skirt, were clearly visible. She described a few circles high above my bed, then, as she approached me, she gradually shrank to the size of a large chicken. She let her broom drop with a clatter and hiked up her skirt with both hands to dash around the room in comical hops shouting *"Csin, Csin gatyás tyúk"* - "Chin, chin, hen in pants! Chin, chin, hen in pants!"

This recurring dream lasted for years, and only started to fade after 1944. By that time, I had grown fond of her and her soft voice, her narrow, freckled face and green eyes behind her thick glasses.

My next teacher of religion in the *gymnasium* was a short and chubby priest with a flat nose who kept a rosary twisted around his fingers at all times. We called him "Pancake Face". The one after him was smart and looked like a filmstar. Yes, he looked like Gregory Peck.

Many of the girls fell in love with him. As he stood tall and lean in his black cassock, we hung on his every word.

I wonder whether my short-lived desire to become a nun was influenced by his magnetic presence?

25

Lust and sloth

We were rigorously prepared in school for our confession before our first Communion.

When to say what. Not to leave out anything. The tall nun made us aware of the sin of lying to God and extolled His generosity. "Your soul will be wiped clean by His hand if you admit to the priest in the confessional what you have done and ask for absolution. You go in, kneel down, lean close to the screen and recite clearly the list of your transgressions. You know the Ten Commandments. You just go down the list and find what applies to you.

"Remember, if you kneel down at the altar to receive Christ without confessing a sin, you commit a new Deadly Sin. And if you die with sins on your soul, you may face eternal damnation."

I studied the helpful list of sins in my white prayer book carefully and decided to confess them all to be on the safe side and avoid leaving the slightest stain on my soul. I also listened carefully to Chin Chin, who added extra sins to my list.

Lust and sloth were the two most confusing sins. I had problems about desiring the wife of my neighbour, although I liked very much the mother of my friend Vica. She baked the most delicious biscuits. But I only desired her biscuits, and never dared to eat enough to be accused of gluttony either.

When I asked Grandma about gluttony, she laughed. "Gluttony? Ha! When you eat like a little bird and you are as skinny as a rail? You must be kidding. Forget about gluttony."

Apu was not too forthcoming about lust. "Excessive desire beyond reason," he said on his way out.

According to Anyu, it was too early for me to worry about lust. But I added it to my list for the priest, just in case I desired something too excessively. Like the crystal paperweight I saw once in the shining vitrine of the Baums. It had a star in the middle and it could splinter the light into a million sparks.

Sloth was confusing because I was sure I was not free of it. Lying on a carpet with my head propped on an elbow, reading a book, was one of my favourite pastimes often interrupted by Grandma: "Get up lazybones, you'll be late."

But then I heard Anyu bragging: "She is full of beans. My daughter is not a bit lazy. When she hikes up the mountains with us, she leads the way, runs ahead."

I came to the conclusion that I should add sloth to the list. And I added that I *paráználkodtam,* which according to the dictionary means that I *fornicated* which also sounded plausible to my unseasoned ears not yet attuned to the ways of mortal sins.

To stand in the long line in front of the heavy curtain of the finely carved confessional among old ladies fingering their rosaries and adult men uneasily shuffling in place, made me feel like a grownup. I was entitled to join them. I could be a sinner taken seriously by the priest.

When it was my turn to enter, I closed the curtain behind me and knelt down close to the grille that hid the priest's face. I read to him the list I penciled the day before with large enough letters to make out in the dim light. I was rewarded with a few words of absolution delivered in a semi-whisper together with the number of prayers I was obliged to say.

I stepped out feeling light, my burden of sins lifted, damnation dodged.

Terra incognita

How could I list all that I do not know?
all that I haven't read
haven't seen
haven't learned
haven't heard
nor understood?

As I grope my way
in the thicket
of this new century
we've named 21st
stepping over
obsolete books
changing maps

hoary theories
and try to grasp
the newly charted
planets of the mind
they speed up my vertigo
as I attempt to go
I don't know
where.

26

Risky tunes

I relished the ribald humour of risky tunes I learned and sang before the war:

Vak Pali
Vak Pali
mindent lát
a kutyának a valagát.

I could drum with my fingers on the table this rhythmic ditty:

tam-tatam, tam-tatam, tam, tam, tam.
tam-tatam, tam-tatam, tam.

Two index fingers tapping, tap-tap-tapping the rhythm of the tune for several minutes without stopping. Of course, I refrained from saying the silly lyrics in front of Anyu. She didn't need to know what I was tapping.

Or in front of Apu.

It would've irritated him, like any other of my prolonged repetitions. "It's not funny! Stop it!"

My funny was vastly different from their funny:

Blind Pali
Blind Pali
sees it all
every dog's asshole
big and small.

In school I picked up other songs, some even worse. I did not know what was wrong with them until much later, when I could detect sexual innuendos. How did I know then not to sing them in "good company"? That's a mystery. But I remember humming them going up and down the steep stone steps to the cellar and singing them aloud to the piles of coal and wood logs smelling of damp rat piss and knowing that they belonged there, that the setting enhanced the songs. Like this one:

Szőr a szitában
kislány az ágyban
hosszában…

Roughly translated:

In the bed
girl athwart
in the sieve
hairs got caught.

Grandmother's favourite was a song not at all funny. It was about forget-me-nots, those shy, unassuming, tiny flowers that bloomed profusely in the wild and in gardens everywhere:

Forget-me-nots
forget-me-nots
bloom along a
steep hillside

I feel poorly
sick with heartache
heading for an early grave

do not forget
my last request:
that for my grave
weave a blue wreath
of forget-me-nots.

Grandma sang this song with a tremulous voice full of feeling. I watched her hands stop working and settle on her stomach in a gesture that seemed to hold her heart from sinking. Feeling uneasy, I thought about our trips to the cemeteries in Pest and Püski, to the many graves of her dead.

Then I wondered why we never took to them bouquets of forget-me-nots. Roses, chrysanthemums, lilies, carnations, lilacs, yes, we took almost everything else. Did she reserve the humble forget-me-not for herself?

27

A Viennese dwarf

Pipsi was a Viennese dwarf pigeon with red feet. Its black feathers were tinged with a dazzling fluorescent green and its wings were black with white polka dots. We could not find out where it was from, although we asked around. I made up a story about a princess locked up in a tower who used it as her postal pigeon to send SOS messages.

It flew in our wide-open window on a summer day before the war and was unable to fly away because Grandma had cut its long wing feathers short, and it gave up trying to rise into the sky. It could only manage to hurl itself short distances upwards from the floor as far as the top of the bookshelf and from there on to the curtain rod, or to its favourite perch on a shoulder, anyone's shoulder.

Its arrival had turned our household upside down, but nobody objected for long when I begged to keep it. I pronounced it a girl and gave her the name of Pipsi.

If you opened your mouth, she went for your teeth, pecking and picking them with unflagging interest. Maybe she thought that they were bits of fresh corn in a row.

There was no such thing in 1942 as bird flu, and I thought nothing about her lumps of shit drying on the shelves, on the spines of books and on the pillows. I was in charge of cleaning up after her, cutting out small squares of cardboard from a shoebox to use as a spatula for scraping up droppings, carefully wiping the remaining smears with a soapy rag. Nothing could dampen my love for Pipsi, for her tilted head as she intelligently scrutinized our comings and goings. Whenever I lay down on my *sezlony*, she would land on my chest and, after a few turns with her tail sweeping across my chin, sit down in front of my face. I can still feel her sharp toenails on my breast, although her whole body was light, mostly feathers. It was impossible not to take notice of her because she interfered with my reading, blocking my view.

On peaceful Sunday afternoons, when the sun poured in the window, and the lilacs in our yellow vase above the bookshelf filled the room with their scent, it was time for our siesta. Each of us grabbed a book. Anyu and Apu lay down on their velvet mattress, stuffed pillows behind their head, and sank into their reading, while in the kitchen Grandma rattled the dishes in a *lavór,* washing up what she had collected from the dining table. I can still see my parents, book in hand, (Apu with a Vicki Baum or Erle Stanley Gardner; Anyu with a Jókai Mór or Stefan Zweig) drowsy with contentment, weighed down by bellyfuls of chicken soup, crumbed *Wiener schnitzel* topped up with slices of sweet walnut tart, or in the spring with Grandma's cherry strudel.

Apu, curled up, with one hand on Anyu's hip, appeared to be in control of the world. There seemed nothing wrong with both of them ignoring Grandma, who was doing what grandmas were born to do in kitchens. Pipsi was part of the picture as she lay asleep on Apu's shoulder, her beak tucked into a wing.

For years she never laid an egg. Grandma voiced her suspicion that she was a he, because it was hard to tell. Then it happened, when fresh eggs were already scarce because of the war, she laid an egg on a dishrag in the kitchen cupboard. Grandma triumphantly carried it into the room to show us. It was a tiny egg, slightly speckled, a perfect miniature miracle.

"How should I cook it?" she asked.

A noisy discussion followed. Soft-boiled? Fried? Scrambled?

We settled on soft-boiled. Grandma served it in an eggcup. Anyu cracked the top and we all had a tiny spoonful. I delayed swallowing my share for a while to remember the taste forever.

Then Anyu said, "We have to be careful. People are hungry. Someone might get the idea to grab her."

It soon happened. Pipsi disappeared.

I went around the house asking people if they had seen someone taking her, but nobody did. Mr Kelemen compiled a list of those who came and went through the gate that day. Grandma and I started to track down each visitor and spent days between air raids trudging through unfamiliar yards in the neighbourhood, climbing stairs in dilapidated apartment houses knocking on doors asking about a lost pigeon.

Finally, we got a lead from an old woman in Tüzér Street. She remembered seeing a bird in her neighbour's kitchen two stories above her flat. I ran up the stairs so fast, Grandma could hardly follow. When a child opened the door, I immediatelyspotted Pipsi on the kitchen floor next to a dish filled with something that looked like porridge. The child, a boy with snotty nose and short fat arms who could not have been more than four years old, started to cry as Grandma scooped up Pipsi.

A tall woman, probably the mother of the boy, kept apologizing and rapidly repeating that her husband found the bird helplessly limping on the ground, no, she didn't know exactly where, but he felt so sorry for the bird and so worried about cats catching it, that he brought it home, and the boy fell in love with this dove, she said, and although they hardly had enough to eat themselves, they fed it and called it Bobo, and Bobo was part of the family now, and they were sorry if that caused us alarm and any trouble, and her husband will also be sad to see Bobo go, not to mention her son, look how he is crying, and if we ever wanted to get rid of the bird, they would be happy to..."

We fled and hurried home.

"They fed her all right," I said almost ready to cry myself as we climbed the stairs.

"They were fattening her for slaughter," Grandma grumbled as she unbuttoned her coat and lifted out Pipsi who lay snug on her familiar bosom.

I thought of the boy and didn't believe her.

Pipsi, definitely fatter, made herself at home again as if nothing had happened. I felt obliged to tell our neighbours the happy news, although they didn't seem to care much.

That evening I went to bed earlier than usual. Rolling over to my back, I opened my favourite Karl May book to read the pages filled with bloody ambushes and ceremoniously smoked peace pipes. Pipsi took up her perch below my chin to share with me the exploits of noble Indian warriors and my wise hero, Old Shatterhand.

Little did I know that in neighbouring Austria, Karl May, who had never seen an Indian, was also the favourite author of a boy who grew up to be Adolf Hitler, the man whom I wanted to kill.

We never found out what happened to Pipsi in the end. During the long siege and incessant air raids, she disappeared again. Probably, she couldn't stand the noise.

28

Living with Bernard Shaw

The paint on the toilet door had interesting patterns. I tried to decipher the puzzles beneath the cracks of the peeling white enamel that covered the yellow undercoat.

I could see swirls resembling writing. "*Jaj*" and "*Ne*", meaning "ouch" and "don't". Not happy words.

And there was the head of G.B. Shaw.

My father often spoke highly of Shaw, telling me that I'd enjoy reading him one day. I think that he aspired to write like him. He showed me his picture, a bearded old man with a kind face. And one day his head, tilted at a mournful, attentive angle, turned up on the lower edge of the toilet door. The discovery pleased me. He became my friend, drawing my eyes as soon as I sat down and reassuring me with his comforting familiarity. His *bons mots*, often repeated by Apu, his cocky remarks made me smile and for a moment forget about the dark window above my head. I tried not to be afraid of him, although his sayings were bordering on sin. I told myself that my personal Shaw, nestled in the familiar curlicues of peeling paint, was a benign person. His contours only rarely changed by Grandma's wet sponge, when she was rubbing the door too hard.

Shaw's head made me forget the hovering ghost in the window. I forced myself to look at him while I listened to the noises behind the door, satisfying sounds: Grandma turning on the groaning tap in the kitchen, a door slamming in the courtyard, laughter and someone shouting "Good morning!" or "Good night!"

The window over my head opened to the *lichthof,* but we never kept it open into that narrow shaft of air shared with another toilet window above us. It was tightly closed, dusty and dim. I would turn on the bare bulb stuck on the ceiling and try to avoid looking at the darkness outside.

It was a small window, but big enough to frame a head, a head looking in, nose pressed to the glass. I didn't see it, but I could feel it there, breathing on the glass behind the dry twigs of geranium Grandma stored in a jar on the windowsill every winter.

I tried not to look at that ghost. He might do something if he knew that I knew that he was lurking there with sunken, baggy eyes under his dark hood. I didn't need to look. I was sure.

I kept my eyes glued on Shaw's scalloped pale yellow beard.

How could I know then, that years later Shaw would re-enter my life bringing trouble? That I would be accused of sacrilege by the parents of a few students in California for teaching Shaw's play *Man and Superman* and speaking of the Devil and Hell in a lighthearted way? For letting them hear *The Statue* describe the Inferno in Act III:

> "Here there is no hope, and consequently no duty, no work, nothing to be gained by praying, nothing to be lost by doing what you like. Hell, in short, is a place where you have nothing to do but amuse yourself."

29

How many lives?

At times I am convinced that I have lived more than one life.

It was another me who was a child before the war. It was an entirely different person who went to university during the Communist era, comfortable in complicity, a self-centered teen, inward looking until 1955.

When all dreams were dashed in 1956 and I arrived in America, I was again a different person, ready to assimilate into a continent offering seemingly limitless possibilities. While I waitressed in Maine, Florida and California, while I studied at Columbia, San Francisco State and UCLA, while I dated various men: Brooklyn lawyer, Baltimore medical student, English mathematician, Japanese student, I gradually opened my mind to the world.

When I worked as a teacher and journalist in California and married and became a mother, I was busy writing and nesting, trying to be useful and at the same time getting absorbed into California's complex society.

And when my husband built a yacht to turn his back on competitive consumerism, to get away from complexity, our son and I joined him to sail to New Zealand at the age of 40.

I became a different person again, going as far away as possible from Budapest in body and in mind.

In New Zealand, distant from crowded continents, we settled in the small village of Russell by the sea.

I learned to become another woman again. I slowed down and was mindful of local lore, of the power of the indigenous population, of

Maori culture, of local history and ecology.

Now, in my 80s when I have more time to think, I am a different person with a different life again, a life seemingly disconnected from the previous ones.

The word *seemingly* is determinal here.

The more I compare my many lives, the more I find the same child lurking in the background. She has been present in the emotions that tipped, and still tip the scales of the choices I make.

Why care about the cosmos?

I am told that I am
a composite of elements.

Part Calcium,
Oxygen, Hydrogen
Phosphorus, Nitrogen
et cetera et cetera
identical to the ashes of glowing
celestial bodies of long ago.

My flesh based on carbon
and on amino acids
is present in the coldest parts
of interstellar space
brewed at the dawn of time
by behemoth explosions of hypernovae.

But why look up?

The sky is way too far when
I need new tires for the car
and there is a sale of duvet covers
in a mall not far.

I haven't got the right PhDs
to let me fathom the mysteries of sub-atom
that make up my toenails and hair.
Hell,
it's easier to turn to Twitter
and learn that Rihanna
started a new trend in beach fashions.
She was last seen
in a modest one piece suit.

30

S-idolatry

I had to rub the brass door handles with my index finger wrapped in a rag that had been dipped into Sidol, a creamy white cleaning fluid. This job was delegated to me way before my school years. I remember needing a stool to reach the higher handles on our windows, starting in the kitchen and proceeding through the hallway to the room and the bathroom. The darkened brass turned white with the thick film I spread with my finger.

I had to wait until it dried, turned into a powdery coat, then I was allowed to rub it off with a dry cloth until it left a shine, pure and clean, the way Grandma wanted it when she came to do her thorough inspection, squinting and smiling if my work was satisfactory.

As I was growing up, I tried even harder, not only because I expected the reward of a slice of apple or a bit of bread and jam. I wanted more. I was after the satisfaction of seeing the shiny brass on doorknobs and on the narrow strips nailed to the thresholds. I wanted to signal that our small, rented space over a factory yard was kept the way it should be: cared for, perfectly clean.

To keep rubbing until the polished metal sparkled was part of a brass-clad order with Grandma in charge.

31

Why? Why?

She often lost her patience trying to answer my questions.

"Why is the flame of the gas stove blue and the flame of the match more yellow?"

"Why do geranium roots have to be put to sleep in winter?"

"Why do cocks crow at dawn?

"Why does Mr Kelemen frisk every worker at the end of the day? And why does Mrs Kelemen check the bras of women in her kitchen before they can go home? I saw her do it!"

Grandma did take the time to answer properly this one. "To make sure that they don't steal from the factory."

"Why do they steal?"

"Some steal because they are bad, others because they are poor."

"Why are they poor?"

"Now I must go down to the cellar and bring up some kindling."

"But why are they poor?"

"That's enough!"

"Are we poor?"

"Stop it!"

32

Uncle Feri

Uncle Feri turned up one day, and someone said (Was it Grandma or was it he, himself, who told me?) that he was Anyu's younger brother.

After that, I saw him arrive at our place unexpectedly once or twice a year to see Grandma.

His face lit up when he saw me, and he would timidly comment on how much I had grown every time. When he touched me, it was always a light hesitant touch on my shoulder as I passed him by in the kitchen where he sat curled up on a *hokedli.* I felt that he loved me from a self-imposed distance, but I didn't know what to say to him, how to overlook his disturbing appearance.

Grandma had taught me not to stare, so I tried to avoid looking at his body and concentrated on his face that was all right under his cap. He was short and misshapen. His shoulders were wide and powerful over a hunchbacked torso clad in a black wool coat he never took off, not even in summer. There was an odour around that coat that I tried to ignore and could not place. It was a mixture of coal dust, stale tobacco and sweat, of alcohol and sour mould.

He quietly answered Grandma's questions, but I never stayed around long enough to find out what they talked about. After he was gone, Grandma's remarks were short and dismissive. It took me years to piece together his life story.

Some old people I knew in the village of Püski told me that he was born a cripple, while others talked about him being beaten and hiding in a shed.

I don't know which version is true.

According to Grandma, he was not as smart as my mother. He dropped out of school because he was bullied and looked for any work he could find. Later he landed a job at an importer firm and worked as a deliveryman distributing exotic fruits like oranges and mandarins from Italy. Sometimes he gave some damaged or overripe oranges to Grandma, things we could not buy on Lehel Market. I remember the sweetness of those.

He married a good woman, said Grandma, putting heavy emphasis on the word good. She was a hard worker sorting damaged fruit in the warehouse, and the boss allowed them to live in a flat on the premises. They had a baby daughter, but his wife died soon of tuberculosis, and he hurriedly married another woman who changed him into an unhappy alcoholic. Grandma refused to see her, holding her responsible for the arrival of a slew of children adding to their poverty.

I never asked Anyu whether she agreed with Grandma. Never learned what she thought of her brother, who found a new job after the war feeding coal to the furnace of the textile factory right across the street from our house. His visits became even less frequent then.

When Grandma died, he turned up at the funeral. He walked up to the open coffin and leaned over her body, rearranged her hair and started stroking her face with the back of his hand. He sobbed when his wife pulled him away. That was the first time I saw her and the half dozen children who stood in the back quietly. All of them had their mother's big dark eyes and heart-shaped face. My cousins. I never learned their names.

I was working in Los Angeles, still a refugee without a passport in 1958, when my mother died. Apu sent me the photos of her funeral. There stood my Uncle Feri in the front row by the open grave and next to him his handsome wife and their children, all of them let into the family on the rare occasions of funerals.

33

Grandma keeps growing

As I entered the stage of grand-motherhood myself and noticed my own changing perspectives, Grandma's image and her power over me magnified in my mind. I was compelled to write poems about our days together.

Granny knots

to secure the warp that holds the loose weft
along the fringes of an old carpet
left over right
right over left

I sort the threads into bundles of three
and bend forward to plait fraying ends
left over right and under
right over left and under

that's when my hands call up grandmother
combing my tangled waist-length brown hair
left over right
right over left

with a needle sharp comb tearing through knots
she tugged and she plaited two tidy *zopfs*
left over right and under
right over left and under

"That hurts!" I'd protest but she kept silent
her face in the glass remained defiant
left over right
right over left

today I wonder what ran in her head
while she pulled and she clasped hand over hand
left over right and under
right over left and under

was it her daily rite, a silent prayer
to impose order layer by layer
left over right
right over left

was she entwining her wishes in strands
and securing each with merciless hands
left over right and under
right over left and under
to protect me from the devil's hot breath
was this her way of care and caress
left over right
right over left

had she envisioned me as a grown woman
making love, giving birth, turning old then

wondered if I would *"remember when"*
left over right and under
right over left and under

Pea Shelling Ritual

It is the tender drumbeat,
the ping-ping of peas,
in the tin bowls
that puts us in tune
as we sit in the sun
outside the kitchen door.

Grandma and I
intent on cracking open the pods
between forefinger and thumb
brush off the soft seeds,
rows of green beads,
that cling to velvet beds.

I hug a bowl between my knees
and glance over to see if
her dish fills faster than mine,
catching her eyes doing the same.

The toccata of tumbling peas
marks the moments
spent on our stools,
the fumble of nimble hands
at play and the promise
of sweet pea soup
with finely chopped parsley
floating in milky sauce
with a dash of paprika for zest.

As the sun slumps west,
our unhinged peas
twirl in the boiling pot
too hot to taste.

34

Novice Mata Haris

To get away with shady acts, to see but not to be seen is an art that needs to be practiced every day. We made sure to practice spying after school almost every day.

Vica, my best friend, and I had at our disposal a perfect practice ground for undercover work: a factory with dozens of workers and office clerks, a front yard and a backyard filled with hiding places, an apartment house up front with eight apartments, not to mention the goings on in the staircase, in the cellars and in the huge washroom stuck under the roof.

Spying was rewarding in more than one way. Hiding made our heartbeat speed up. We held our breath as we watched people practicing their secret vices that ranged from nose-picking, crotch-scratching, quarrelling, dressing and undressing and sometimes even snooping around just like we did. Then we had to report to each other whatever we spotted. For that, we had to find a safe place where nobody could hear us, not even when we used our secret *turgudorgodsz* language. For a while, we also took notes and carefully assigned numbers to people in order to avoid detection in case our notes were discovered.

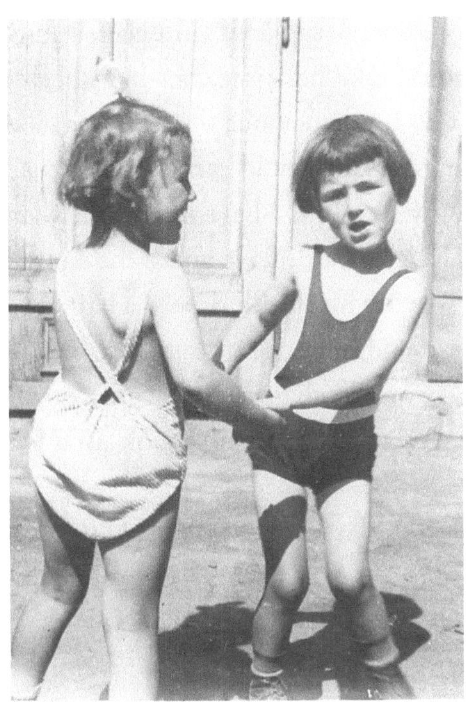

Vica was Number 1, I was Number 2, Mr Kelemen was Number 3, Mrs Kelemen Number 4 and so on.

"Number 1 reports to 2:

4 shouts to 3 to bring in more coal. 3 shouts back "in a minute" then says under his breath "more coal, more coal, more coal... shut up". Number 3 proceeds along the yard with empty bucket and goes down to the cellar."

Mr Kelemen was not the only one who talked to himself while he was walking around. In the stairwell, as they rushed up and down, all our neighbours said funny things.

Paula, the Baum's maid who was Number 5, rattled off unconnected words: "Cottage cheese, bleach, lentils, soap, wax, yeast, brown shoe polish, a dozen eggs." I scribbled it all down faithfully as I tiptoed after her.

Mrs Kostos, Number 8, spoke in sentences, but those were equally puzzling. She would take her time, her high heels going clop-clop on top of each step. It was obvious that she was talking to her white poodle. But what she said would rarely make sense to a dog: "No, no, I won't go. Why should I? I have my mother here. How could I? Stop it, don't do it here, wait till we get to the street. I can't leave her. Don't pull. He's wasting his breath. I need a haircut. It's easy for him. His mother is dead and buried. I must stay firm."

She would carry on like that, while I would press close to the wall of the staircase, staying invisible. She took up a lot of space in my notebook.

Mr Kostos never said a word as he rushed up and down swinging his arms.

"Number 1 reports that Number 8..."

Then there was our vice-concierge, who was in charge of rubbish collection and washing the entrance and the stairwell. She was a big, busty woman who lived alone next to the upstairs washroom.

Tall like a man, she carried the broom, the mops and the heavy buckets of soapy water with ease. Her name was Antonia, but Vica and I called her Miau, because she had three cats.

It was not easy to avoid her on the staircase because she often walked barefoot, while everyone else came noisily, giving us time to run ahead or follow behind. She didn't talk much. Sometimes she sang funny songs while she scrubbed the steps:

"The hut's burning
sizzling the thatch
ignore the blonde
grab the brunette..."

She stopped as soon as somebody went by. If we said good morning, she would nod without smiling.

After the war I learned that she was the one who saved young Mr Baum by hiding him in her room from the spying eyes of the Arrow Cross men.

35

A bas-relief

Apu came home one evening with a small package wrapped in newspapers and tied with a string.

"Come and see what I've got," he shouted, as he made his usual grand entrance throwing his hat on the table and his coat on a chair. "It's from a famous sculptor, and I traded it for a book."

"Which book?" Anyu asked.

"*From Beggar to Prince*, that's what he asked for. He is related to a character in one of my stories."

"Which one?"

"Not the beggar and not the prince, but the actress."

Through the years, Apu always managed to get things in exchange for his books, not paying money for the odd ticket to movies, to theatres and soccer matches, even for toys that I could choose in the toy warehouse of an old friend of his. He took me there one day and told me that I could have anything I see. Shelves reaching up to the ceiling were full of treasures: giant teddy bears, tricycles, music boxes, dolls of all sizes, electric trains, and toy villages. I chose a wood duck, a shiny yellow pull toy that followed me everywhere at the end of a string in my hand.

What did he bring us this time?

We gathered around the table and stood watching him unwrap the package. Grandma kept wiping her hands, quite cross that she was summoned from the kitchen. Anyu leaned back on a chair possibly enjoying the theatrical moment, while I was holding my breath expecting a present for me, for me alone.

What emerged was a framed brass bas-relief, no bigger than an average size book. At first sight, it seemed to depict a bunch of swimmers in turbulent waves, maybe doing backstrokes in such tight proximity that they had to be kicking each other.

"Nice," said Grandma and hurriedly retreated into the kitchen.

Father held it up towards the lamp and, as the light fell on it at an angle, I could see clearly that there was something wrong.

"Horrible," Anyu whispered.

I stared at the faces. Open-mouthed faces. Hair spread out like mown grass on the water. And there were the hands. Lots of hands reaching towards the sky. Not swimming hands. Drowning hands.

"Ujvidék," Apu said. "1942. We were good at shooting people into the Danube."

"Who?" I asked. "Who did it?"

"Do we have to..." Anyu started.

"She should know," Apu cut in as he turned towards me. "Yes, your daughter is old enough to know what has gone on by the banks of this icy river."

Anyu got up and left the room.

I did want to know.

Apu and I found a nail, and we hung the bas-relief above a shelf. It fitted well next to a drawing of a half-naked woman. A towering beauty, she was standing below a castle wall watching two muscular men engaged in a sword fight. Her robe exposed one breast and her left thigh and knee, but not her left foot tangled in the drapery of what looked like a torn toga ready to fall open all the way. The men were young and statuesque like her, but fully dressed in tight-fitting trousers and open-necked shirts. For a while, I dreamed of growing up to be a woman like her, straight and proud, a woman who inspired men to fight and die for her.

Now, next to the bas-relief, she suddenly seemed insignificant against the drowning faces gasping for air.

"Ujvidék," said Apu. "A mass murder. They lined them up on the shore and shot them into the Danube. This river has witnessed such a lot of unspeakable barbarity... One day you'll learn about it. One day, maybe, you can figure out why do people..." he handed me the hammer, and I put it down on the bed.

"Who did it?" I asked again.

Just then, Anyu entered the room smiling with a plate of freshly baked *pogácsa*. "Since you got us a new work of art, let's celebrate. Come to the table and sit down," she said, and I followed biting into one snatched from the plate.

Nothing could surpass the taste of a *töpörtyűs pogácsa*. It melted in my mouth. Grandma made it with crackling. The fresh hot *pogácsa* absorbed the fat from the broken crackling and tasted salty and moist.

Anyu won.

Apu gave up on the story of the bas-relief, although I wanted to know more. He kept quiet. When I asked later, he told me that it was unspeakable.

Today Ujvidék is Novi Sad, part of Serbia, and its history in Wikipedia mentions the massacre of 1942, the subject of the bas-relief.

The line-up

when the men come
to search us
to herd us
who'll hide me

when they make us
go to the wall
who will stand
before me?

when they shout
raise your hands
who will be
next to me

when they aim
guns at us
will Father
cover me

when they pull
the trigger
will he shield me

will he hide
me under
his body

and whisper
play dead child
play dead to
stay alive

36

Windy Novembers

When I was born, grandma's hair had already turned salt-and-pepper brown, almost grey. But according to an old photo, it was still thick and long, tightened into a bun on the back of her neck. Later, and that is how I remember her myself without the aid of photographs, her hair was white and short, combed straight back from her face and forehead and secured with a round comb on her nape. I suspect that she used to cut it herself, as it was always the same length, always flat and neat, never a strand out of place.

She knew so many people I didn't know, and also knew how everyone was related to everyone else way back, for generations, even before she herself was born.

She would say befuddling things like: "Your great-great-aunt Etus in the 1880s married John from Bodak who was related by marriage to my grandfather's brother-in-law. May they all rest in peace."

It seemed to me that most of her relatives and acquaintances lived in cemeteries. Some important ones in Rákoskereesztúr, many others in Püski and Moson.

I didn't mind going to the Rákoskeresztúr cemetery with Grandma although getting there was an ordeal we repeated every November.

Rákoskeresztúr

Potted chrysanthemums fill the string bag
pressing against my ribs
on the crowded streetcar
as it squeals around the curves
past the brewery beyond the slums,
past the monumental masons' yards
filled with stone angels
and black marble obelisks.

Look ahead and keep your face turned
towards the sky, says Grandma
as she hangs by a strap.
No seats on the tram to the cemetery.
It's All Saints' Day.

I try to gulp air to keep my nausea at bay,
search for the sky between two elbows
and the hip of a heavy widow in black
who is staring down a man
steadfastly refusing to offer his seat.

Take a deep breath, says grandmother
who wears grey not the black
that goes with fresh death
and who asked me last night
as she tucked me into bed,
"When I'll be dead,
will you miss me? Will you be sad?"

We pass through a huge iron gate
and hurry along the carriageway
under half-naked chestnut trees
ankle deep in brittle leaves stirred
by the chill wind that whistles and hoots
among the mausoleums of the rich
as we make our way to the back rows
where they lay the less grand dead.

I hug the chrysanthemums
and inhale their pungent scent,
rub my nose in the soft petals
trying to keep up with grandmother's back
while the hypnotic drone
of a small plane lowers
from the sky above
dark with threatening snow.

First to Grandpa.
I pick weeds at his feet while
she lights a candle inside a tin
but the wind makes it gasp and gutter.
I hear her mutter prayers as she rests her hand
over the wood cross bearing his name.
I try to recall in vain his face, his voice.
She puts a flower over a neglected grave
next to his, but we don't weed that one.

Carrying on further to the rear
where children's graves sag
under rampant grass
we find the infant whom
she lost to scarlet fever one winter
after my mother was born.

His lopsided cross is hard to spot in a
tangled corner where a runaway
climbing rose grabs my shoulder
to hold me, trap me, keep me
until I cry out and she turns and
pulls the thorns off my back.

Next comes her sister who died giving birth.
Her iron name plate has gone to rust.
The last flowers we tie to her cross.

Then we sit down on a bench marked
"In Memoriam"
of a brave general killed in some war
and eat smoked bacon sandwiches
with pickled cucumbers, slaking
our thirst with water from a dripping tap
by a heap of mouldering bouquets

crumpled crepe ribbons and wilted wreaths
while the ever-present doleful drone
of that lone plane lingers overhead.

37

Grandma's spooky friends

Grandma's living acquaintances were a motley crowd. I've met a few of them.

Why were they so strange?

Why did Grandma keep them in the kitchen, never inviting them into the room? Why did they whisper hunched over the table holding a coffee mug in one hand and a handkerchief in the other? Why did they stop talking whenever I came close?

One couple never came, but we visited them a few times. I don't remember the name of the narrow street somewhere in the 6th District where we walked up a dark staircase to their door.

The woman Grandma called Iluska must have been my mother's age. She was so thin, her dress hung on her without any suggestion of a body underneath. Her face was narrow, her mouth a thin line that only became visible when she opened it to speak. I could hardly hear what she said because her slurred syllables seemed to emerge from under water. She scared me, although she offered me a slice of bread spread with butter and honey and kept stroking my hair in an absentminded manner while she mumbled and sighed.

Her husband, whose name I forgot, scared me even more, even though I never laid eyes on him. He was always hiding behind a curtain in the dim kitchen, and I listened to his coughing, a dry barking cough that was as unceasing as his wife's whispers. I gathered gradually that her conversation centred around her own health, threatened by a weak heart since her birth, and around the tuberculosis of her husband gradually deteriorating to the stage of more and more blood in his spit.

Grandma recommended garlic, her usual medication for most conditions. While she talked, Iluska listened leaning towards her, kept nodding, and her thin lips and nose moved in a way that reminded me of pet mice sniffing for food.

When we left and were descending the staircase, I tried to practice a sniffing mouse face, and when we got home I dashed into the bathroom to check out my performance in the mirror.

38

Learning about tact

Before the war, old Mrs Baum was going blind.

"Sugar illness," they said.

The household whispered around her. That was the custom around bedridden people, as if any noise would have delayed their recovery.

"Rest! Stay still! Save your energy. Don't get up. I'll bring it to you." Kind words prompted by compassion surrounded the sick.

Kitty Baum, old Mrs Baum's granddaughter, was a year older than me. Her family owned the house and the factory, and she had become my friend. She lived a floor above me and was busy with tutors and with her nanny. She was often away, travelling somewhere, so we rarely could play together.

She didn't particularly like to visit her sick grandmother in her hushed and roller-blinded bedroom. Sometimes she asked me to go along to keep her company.

On one such occasion, the nurse was still in the room. Kitty should not have barged in without knocking, but when Paula, the maid, opened the front door, she didn't ask us to wait, so Kitty flung open the bedroom door with her usual brusqueness.

In the half-light of the room we saw the nurse bent over the bed, the covers folded back over a tiny body stretched out with the back facing us. Mrs Baum's white skin was visible from the knees up to her waist. It sharply contrasted with the dark blue uniform of the nurse who was pushing an injection into her flesh.

There was no way for us to retreat.

The nurse was a formidable woman of great height and weight with a narrow forehead under a black braid crowning her head. Her arms moved swiftly as she rolled down the nightgown over the pale body, pulled up a red comforter and rearranged the stack of pillows under her patient's head.

Then she turned around to face us.

"Don't stay long. She is tired," she said firmly. I watched her pick up a roll of cotton wool, a syringe and some bottles, stuff them into a box and depart without a backward glance.

"How're you Gran?" Kitty sat down on the edge of the bed. I stood behind her searching for a sign of embarrassment on the face of the old woman. There was a faint smile around her thin lips, and her eyes were wide open. They were big and dark under the half-moon arcs of equally dark eyebrows. All other features seemed to be subordinate to those intense eyes. She was looking at Kitty and ignoring me.

"How was school," she asked without answering her question.

"No school, it's still summer holiday," Kitty said.

"Oh, of course, it must be summer," she said.

I found this amazing. She didn't know that it was summer. What else didn't she know?

"Do you know what day it is?" I asked her.

She turned towards me. "What did you say?"

"Or what month it is?"

"Month? What month?"

"I mean what is the date today? Which year?"

She kept silent and closed her eyes. Her head rolled towards the window and her right hand rose from under the white sheet and waved towards us a dismissive wave.

"Go! Go girls! Go away!"

Kitty rose and lowered her head. "I'll be back tomorrow."

I never went with her again, and when I told Grandma what happened, she was more furious with me than when she had caught me lying about a broken jar of jam.

The unusual harshness of her voice stayed with me through the years.

"You must learn to shut your mouth. Must think before you open it. You were cruel and stupid."

I went into the bathroom and without turning on the light sat on the edge of the tub, my sulking retreat, until Anyu got home.

She was of no help. Tired, as always, she sat down beside me, kicked off her shoes and rubbed her sore feet.

"I am surprised," she said. "This was not like you. Not at all. You must learn that words can be more wounding than a sharp knife."

Mother's song

The rent is due.
I am late for work.

There is soot on the windowsill.
And the floor needs wax.
The radio is spouting propaganda,
but don't say that at school.
You must give fresh water to the flowers
and when you go by the Kendes,
knock on the door
and hand in this plate of cake.

For God's sake,
hold your head high,
don't go into dark alleys,
but never turn away
from a pleading hand
and always listen
to the pigeons in the park.

39

Words from a deep well

My mother's voice. She is arguing with my father. I hear their voices rising above the usually calm and steady sounds they use when they carefully explain something to me. Father's voice comes through the bathroom door as short clipped sounds thrown in anger. He is the louder one. Mother's voice is softer, higher pitched. Those voices are real, coming from a deep well of memory filled to the brim with floating phrases.

"We must pay the gas first. You know we are late already." I hear Anyu firm and pleading at the same time.

"Tibor didn't pay me. What the devil should I do?" Apu doesn't expect an answer. He hurls the words.

"You must go and ask…"

"Wait till next week."

"Next week. Next week may be too late." Anyu almost whispers.

"I don't want to hear."

"We must put the sheets in again then. And you must take back this perfume to Lieberman's."

"I can't ever please you."

"Not when you splurge, when we need every fillér."

"I am always wrong, damn it."

"Did I say that?"

"When I buy you something because I..."

And about here, I know that he will embrace her.

Soon I would have to go with Grandma to the pawnshop with a pile of sheets and pillowcases again. Loaded down going, empty-handed coming home.

40

Underfoot

From toddlerhood to early adolescence Vica Bauer was my closest friend. Literally. She lived with her mother, father and grandfather across the yard from me, and I met her every day. We enjoyed a seemingly boundless universe of corners and steps, ladders and staircases, rooftops and barrels of oleanders, attics and cellars, humming machinery and idling delivery trucks. And we could explore all of it with impunity.

The house was used to us, two small girls, awkward and nosy pre-schoolers to start with, running around. Not naughty boys, but girls who had learned by the time they were let loose in the factory yard how to say thank you and how to curtsy.

We were tolerated if we got in the way, warned, even shouted at sometimes, but with a smile mitigating the gruff voice.

Children. Underfoot.

Hide and seek involved squeezing between bales of wool, squatting on the roof of an adjoining building, kneeling behind a mountain of black briquettes or by the stacked cages of watchful egg-laying hens.

There was so much to see, to learn, to touch, to smell: wet wool, feathers, planks full of sharp splinters, hard steel steps, narrow stone steps, creaking wooden ladders, horses and butterflies.

And there were a startling variety of adults to figure out. Some ignored us because we were not important, others were reminded of their own childhood and came outside to lean on the rail and watch us climb, jump and burst into places where no adult would be caught treading.

41

Turgudorgodsz

Vica and I are sitting on the cement steps in front of their door. We are talking fast, so fast, my tongue trips over itself. The sun is shining, and bees are buzzing among the purple flowers of the lilac bushes planted under the factory windows.

I am hugging my knees, my skirt pulled down to my ankles and I am loud, louder than the spinning machines behind my back that raise their decibels when Vica's father pops the steel door open and stands behind us trying to catch a breath of fresh air free from the fuzz of wool yarn and the smell of lubricating oil.

We carry on talking in the rattling secret language we know he doesn't understand. It makes it possible to say anything and everything we wouldn't dare to say otherwise in front of adults. We love to swim in the waves of sounds and revel in the rhythmic cascade based on the repetition of added syllables that obscure the meaning of words. Here is an example in Hungarian:

"Turgudorgodsz irgigy bergeszérgélnirgi?

This question, a mere opening to clandestine conversations, in English:

Canger yourgoo speargik thirgis waregay?

Which simply means: "Can you speak this way?"

If you practice, you can do it even faster than your normal, everyday speech.

And you end up with giggles and hiccups.

Vica's father makes a dismissive move with his hand coupled with a headshake and goes back into the humming factory.

Having made sure that nobody is looking, we climb up the rickety wooden steps leading to an attic bordering the roof of the DKW-BMW building next door. We step over a low rail. It is so easy to trespass, and it is deliciously hot up there on the flat roof covered with thick rubbery sheets smelling of melting tar that transfers the heat of the sun to the soles of our sandals. They soon get stuck in the soft black goo as we squat down to hide behind the parapet while we survey the street below.

We can endure this only for a short time, but endure we do for the sake of using the malleable tar to fashion small black balls. We line them up and when we have enough for an attack, we aim towards the window displaying the shiny new German cars and watch with delight as some of the tar manages to stick to the glass.

We can't use up more than a dozen, because one of the salesmen soon hears the smack of our artillery and comes out to scan the street.

By the time he thinks to look up, we are safely down the wooden stairs, sitting back on the steps, scraping off the tar from our sandals and continuing our coded dialogue.

"Tharget wargas furgan."

I must get rid of the tar before Grandma looks at my sandals and starts asking questions.

My other grandmother, Ómama, never asks questions or tries to correct me.

42

Ómama's realm

Ómama lost two children. Father was her only surviving child by the time I was born. I was her only grandchild.

My two grandmothers were similar in many ways, both treating me well, but I noticed early that in many ways they were different. Since I attempted to find out about Ómama's past, the differences became clear. To trace her early years was almost impossible by the time I started searching. She remained an enigma, but she gained more and more hold on my imagination.

43

Staying away

Gizella Petyán was born in 1873. I don't know exactly where. She died in Budapest in 1947, two years after my father found her half-dead in the Budapest ghetto.

As a child, it didn't strike me as unusual that Ómama never crossed our threshold. I didn't ask why my father alone took me to visit her. Not Anyu, not Grandma, only Apu, who took a lot of pictures of the two of us. Some of those I still have hanging on the wall in New Zealand.

44

Dimples and wrinkles

"She has my dimples," Ómama pointed proudly at Apu's photos. That's how I learned that when she was young, before dimples turned into wrinkles, her face was similar to mine.

She never told me where she was born or to whom. Her mother and father were never mentioned when I spent lazy summer afternoons with her soaking up the sun in Szent István Park, where she sat on a bench under the trees while I made mud cakes in my favourite sandpit alongside squabbling fellow toddlers.

Luckily, sometime later she dropped some crumbs of information, a few of which stuck. These had to do mostly with losses. There were vague references to a country pub somewhere. Then in no particular order came a coffee house, a green grocery, an apron business and a boarding house.

Most of these referred to her attempts to make a living in Budapest before, during and after the prolonged turmoil of the First World War and the doomed revolution and counter-revolution in its wake.

What made me imagine that she was born into a country pub run by her father?

It is a name. Just this name: Palásti.

The name father chose as his pen name. He must have known.

When I close my eyes, I can see her sweeping the floor in her father's white-washed adobe pub in Palást. Throwing grain from her lifted apron for the chickens running towards her from all corners of the yard. Polishing brass candlesticks. I see her as a tall girl behind the counter smiling at customers and wiping off the wet rings left by their glasses on the countertop. I see her as she dries beer mugs and turns around to replace them on a shelf.

She is still slender, not what my father, her impudent but loving son, called her later, when after her pregnancies, she had become "koca mama", a "sow mama" with a litter of three.

My father's nickname creations were witty, but at times brutal.

The publican's daughter was young and naïve, knew little beyond the house and the village. She had learned how to cook for a crowd of people, how to sew and cut patterns, how to keep books and recite prayers. My imaginary Ómama was a diligent child, eager to help her mother tend to her younger sister, Berta, and her two brothers, Ármin and Béla.

All three of them were to emigrate later to America in search of work and opportunity while they were young.

They must have done well there, because they sent hefty packages of gifts, toys and clothes that Ómama cut up and refashioned into dresses for me. They wrote upbeat letters regularly, first from New York and Chicago, then Maine, Florida and finally from California.

Their names I remember well, because Ómama talked about them a lot and because much later I met Uncle Ármin.

Béla and Berta were dead by the time I arrived in America in 1957.

Before the war, I did see Ómama light *Shabbat* candles on Friday nights and silently and ceremoniously place them on the windowsill. I was too intent on watching her prepare my meal to ask about the meaning of her silence.

She kept quiet about her Jewish faith in front of a granddaughter who was being raised by the other grandmother as a Roman Catholic.

45

Toye Moye Dushinka

Ómama is asking me to raise my arms. She is pulling down a soft pink cloud of a dress over my head. My thumb gets caught in the sleeve. I cry out, and she frees my thumb and helps my head through the neckline, tugs on the back to make the shoulders settle where they are supposed to sit and pushes me away with both hands gripping my wrists to survey me at arm's length. Not bad, she says, satisfied with her work.

I enjoy being a doll, standing straight while she marks the hem, lifting an arm and feeling the tickle of scissors as she widens the hole under my armpit, inhaling deeply to extend my chest so that she can be sure to leave enough room for me to grow for another year. She dresses me in silk and wool, in cotton and linen. I am her model and pride.

When she calls me *toye moye dushinka*, I don't know the words she says, but I know what she means: I am her little treasure, I am her soul. She is using Slovak, the language of her childhood neighbourhood.

As I stand letting her dress and undress me, I am unaware of the unspoken competition between my two grandmothers, both seamstresses on a professional level. It is a competition to please me and to show their love through the products of their respective Singer sewing machines with identical foot pedals, iron wheels and swiftly stabbing needles.

46

Ómama's elegance

When she planned to meet her friends on a park bench or in a café, she always dressed to the hilt. A fine wool coat with a big fur collar in winter. A light silk frock and a neat hat in summer. All the ladies sat in a row on a St Stephen Park bench keeping an eye on us grandchildren playing our awkwardly well-behaved games under their supervision.

As soon as we arrived back at her place, off went the finery to be stored in a wardrobe alongside mothballs and neatly folded linen. Out came a cotton dress and apron. Hands washed, she was ready to cook for me.

Her dresses and aprons were more colourful than Grandma's. More city bright. Grandma's were darker, more country.

To my eyes, both were just right.

47

The ghosts of grandfathers

I remember my grandmothers.

Grandma and Ómama.

They lived longer than my two grandfathers, Grandpa and Ópapa.

48

Ópapa

Ópapa, my father's father, was called Miksa Szilágyi.

He died before I was born. Apu said once that he died after an "old man's operation" when the surgeon left something - a knife? a needle? a glove? - in his belly and sewed him up. It went septic, and by the time they noticed it, it was too late.

I imagined all sorts of needles and knives and settled on the meat knife Grandma used to cut up chickens after she slit their throat. It was a long, sharp knife with a wooden handle, and I saw it resting among the bowels of Ópapa causing acute discomfort and eventual death. His bowels I modeled after the ones Grandma used to tip into the garbage, thin purplish coils scooped out of chickens. These were the only images inspired by Ópapa whom I had never met.

Ómama never showed me a picture of him and never talked about him either.

Much later I learned that he deserted her for a richer woman while their three children were still alive.

Uncle Ármin, one of Ómama's brothers, who was still alive in California when I landed there in 1958, told me a story about his sister's predicament. She asked him to go with her to the fancy place of the new wife and request some money for the children's schooling.

"We rang the bell, and a maid wearing a white headdress and apron came to the door. Ómama asked to talk to the master of the house. The maid said that nobody was at home. We could hear voices and laughter behind the door."

Uncle Ármin told me that the same thing happened before and once more again. "The maid had been instructed not to let us in. Your grandfather knew that she went there to ask for money. She lowered herself to begging for the children's sake."

49

What about Miksa Szilágyi?

My interest in my father's forebears increased with the years when I learned about the influence genes may have on our lives.

Because I thought that Ómama came from Palást, a village in the area of Ipolyság that now belongs to Slovakia, I searched for her husband's family name there on the list of Jews exterminated in German camps, but I found not a single Szilágyi.

Where did he come from?

Next I asked myself another question. How did my grandparents meet if no Szilágyi family lived in Palást and its surroundings?

Well, easily, I reassured myself. The answer did not require too much imagination. Many transient guests must have come through the village to stop for a drink in her family's old pub.

Travelers on horseback. Or coming by on foot.

On foot? No, not my Ópapa.

He had to be more prosperous, more elegant. He must have hitched rides on peasant carts. I see him step off with a suitcase full of merchandise, straighten his coat and dust off his hat that he would wear at a rakish angle.

So in the 1890s, by chance, enters a dashing dandy, a traveling salesman from Budapest. He sits down near the counter, orders a drink and eyes the girl who is standing behind the counter and is rocking to sleep a child in her arms. He takes note of her round face and dimpled smile. He is not averse to the charms of women. He is on his way to become my grandfather.

What can he promise her beside eternal love?

City life? Paved streets and elegant restaurants with white damask tablecloths and silver saltshakers. The Budapest Zoo, the Dunakorzó, the fabulous promenade by the river where well-dressed Sunday women compete to show off the latest fashions, women whose style has earned the city the name "Paris by the Danube".

With three babies in quick succession Gizella had no time to promenade. Miksa was away a lot, chasing business (and women), but kept telling her that he would soon make a big break, luck was just around the corner. He borrowed to start a coffee house, a promising new venture surely, and she was enlisted to cook. They invested in crockery and the fabled white damask tablecloths, but the guests failed to come and sit down at their tables. Unemployment gripped the country. While Gizella's siblings emigrated to America. Gizella didn't move. She was married already. Pregnant. She remained with her Miksa, trying to stay afloat.

My father was Ómama's youngest child. He mentioned to me only once that he had a sister and a firstborn brother. That was when he led me through what seemed to be endless rows of graves in the Jewish cemetery of Rákoskeresztúr talking about his childhood. I didn't pay much attention to what he said about a boy and a girl I didn't know. It was awkward standing there in the damp scrub staring at lopsided headstones covered with fallen leaves while he was scrubbing away mossy stains to reveal the remnants of a foreign alphabet, not at all like the one I was starting to learn.

He told me that both of them died suddenly. I was scared when he mentioned contagious childhood diseases. I think it was scarlet fever for her and diphtheria for him. The possibility of dying young stuck in my mind. I saw them sitting on a cloud above their graves. Heaven was a place where children went, according to Grandma. There was no hunger or cold, and good children grew wings attached to their shoulder blades.

Apu stood for a long time in front of his father's gave. I could read the Hungarian part of the inscription several times: "Szilágyi Miksa – 1869 – 1930 - Mourned by his widow, his son and brothers".

Studying history years later, I was reading about the flood of Slavic and Germanic names "Magyarized" in the 19th and early 20th centuries by citizens wanting to assimilate into Hungarian society. I started to question the origin of Szilágyi, a name I had never questioned before.

I managed to arrive at a tentative conclusion with the posthumous assistance of my sophisticated Aunt Bözsi.

I am the bearer

I am the bearer of unspeakable secrets.
I am the teller of unbearable truths.
I am a grower of redder than red roses.
I am a pusher of stolen goods in pubs.
I am a father who abuses his sons.
I am a joker who never wins a laugh.
I am the woman who does it for a price.
I am the blind man who dreams about the stars.
I am a fanatic in a bulletproof vest.
I am the general who stamps out unrest.
I am a professor stifled by stiff taboos.
I am the priest who prays to lift the clouds.
I am a child who thumbs his nose.
To be a writer I must be all of those.

50

Tiny Francophile Auntie Bözsi

As I grew and became aware of a wider world somewhere "out there" beyond the reduced boundaries of Hungary, I acquired an appetite for

French. Apu had a cousin called Bözsi, who lived a few blocks away. I started French lessons in her apartment overlooking Szent István Park.

It was just a short walk away from our place, but it seemed to be in another world, far from textile factories, smoking chimneys, delivery trucks and lumberyards. Aunt Bözsi's house sat in a manicured park tended by an elderly attendant, whose long stick with a sharp nail at its end would pick up stray pieces of paper and cigarette butts littering the gravel paths. The house, alongside a row of other elegant houses only slightly marked by bullet holes, had several storeys with small balconies facing the trees and the Danube.

As I entered through a swinging door with its curved bronze handle, I knew that this was a step up, something to wish for. The elevator worked. The third floor landing had four doors. One of them was hers. When I rang the bell, an eye looked through a tiny magnifying glass embedded in the middle of the door to decide whether to let me in or not.

Auntie Bözsi was a tiny woman with a determined manner. She moved fast and spoke clearly with clipped words that kept pace with her bobbing permed curls as she nodded rapidly when I pronounced "l'amour dans les ruines" or "trajectoire de la Terre" properly.

Her entry hall was crowded with shelves and upholstered chairs making navigation towards her room difficult. She explained that these acted as barricades against her flat mate, who had been forced upon her by postwar edicts necessary because of the paucity of housing, 'une situation malheureuse', she had to suffer. I learned that the flat mate was a bald man who occupied her second bedroom, and that he often entertained female guests who carelessly left "objectionable objects" drying in the communal bathroom.

She must have told me how she survived the war, but I forgot. She never entered our less opulent apartment, because father never invited any of his relatives.

She talked about her life in Paris, the important people she saw there, and what Endre Ady, whose poems I had to learn by heart in school, said to her once when they met by chance in a restaurant.

I loved sitting in the sun by her round table, perusing a thick volume of *Petit Larousse*, drinking her hot chocolate and listening to the tales of Paris. The sweet bonbons she presented in a lacquered bowl were a plus.

It was Bözsi, my Francophile aunt, who had come to my aid with her family name. Being a spinster, content with non-binding Parisian affairs, she retained her maiden name: Erzsébet Sonnenfeld.

Now, if she was born a Sonnenfeld and never changed her name, I reasoned, then clearly my grandfather was also a Sonnenfeld, furthermore most name changes had clung to the same initials. It may be that my errant grandfather (or perhaps earlier, a great-grandfather?) was originally a Sonnenfeld.

Were there any Sonnenfelds and Petyáns living around Palást?

Long ago, back in the 19th century, did Ómama marry a Sonnenfeld or a newly-minted Szilágyi?

It took me many decades to make up my mind and embark on a pilgrimage to Palást in order to search for their traces.

51

But why Palást?

My fixation on Palást started early in life. It had to do with the many name changes I went through by the age of ten. From Szilágyi to Palásti and from Panni to Éva while I was in school. It didn't stop there: in my 20s from Éva to Barbara in America and then back to Éva and, finally, to Panni again whenever I visited my relatives in Hungary.

52

Crossing relaxed borders

During my visit to Hungary in 2005, my old high school friend Baba offered me and our friend Vali a ride in her car to Slovakia.

Crossing the border was easy. By then both countries were supposed to behave as bona fide members of the European Union, the hopeful alliance formed to bury the old historic rivalries that had culminated in the carnage of two world wars.

It was a humid and cloudy summer day. We were three women tight in a small car rolling out of the dense traffic of Budapest, three old classmates from the 1940s, ex-pupils of *Ráskai Lea Gimnázium.*

By then in our 70s, having matured into a physician, a textile expert, and a writer, we chatted about the price of gasoline, about grandchildren, the vagaries of history, about airfares, and the best recipe for walnut cake. We gossiped about long dead teachers and still living friends, about a classmate who moved to Brazil and another one who struck it rich through two profitable divorces in California.

I was busy amusing my friends by quoting an old xenophobic proverb I was taught as a child in Püski: "Adj a tótnak szállást, kiver a házból." Roughly translated: "Offer a Tót shelter, and he will chase you out of your house." "Tót" was the old, unflattering name of our Slavic neighbours in Slovakia.

We glanced out the window at the flashing landscape: river, trees, tenement houses, trucks, cornfields and castles on hills, always on hills. I tried to imagine Palást, a place that in my mind had grown into the legendary settlement that gave me my name.

There must still be the tavern Ómama talked about, and there must be old people who can recall a family by the name of Petyán. I had no illusions about finding relatives alive, but thought of gravestones overrun by weeds, dating back way before the days of Hitler.

If I had researched Palást, I would have known more, but I always believed in raw first impressions unpolluted by mythology and untainted by commercial or political expediency. Feeling uneasy, I tried to subdue my apprehensions by telling myself that I was entitled to approach strangers and ask probing questions equally uncomfortable for me and the questioned. Questions about a past that, I presumed, people were trying to forget.

I was a tourist stepping out of a new car with a Hungarian license plate. Turning to Baba, I said, "Imangine! I could have been born here."

Palást, now called Plastovce, turned out to be a quiet place.

We saw a fertile valley dominated by its Roman Catholic church, an imposing building on the top of a hill. We parked beside it under a shady tree and entered it, impressed by its size and its tidy interior dominated by a painting above the altar depicting Saint George on his horse, his arm raised ready to slay a fierce dragon.

An elderly caretaker appeared. Obviously proud of his job, he welcomed us speaking Hungarian. He talked about the history of the church. We learned that Pál Palásthy, the bishop of Esztergom, consecrated it in 1898. One of his noble forebears supposedly had been valiant Bors himsself, who fought in the Crusades with King Endre the Second, and the king gave him the whole valley as a reward for his services rendered in 1217.

A templom utca és a Szentháromság 1937 - ben

Recent archeological digs in the area reached back even further, unearthing rich ceramic finds that proved the presence of settlements in the Bronze Age.

When the conquering Hungarians, having arrived from Asia in the 10th century, descended into the valley of the Ipoly River, they found the Bulgarian Chief Zalán ruling the area, according to the 12th century manuscript of the medieval chronicler Anonymous.

I didn't dare to interrupt the friendly caretaker until we had gone around the nave twice, studying each detail. As we stepped outside, he pointed out the local museum below the church, and before we left him, I asked whether he recalled the names of some Jewish families who lived in Palást before the Second World War.

"Yes," he said, "I remember one family. The father was trading rabbit skins. He perished." He could not remember the name of the family just then. "Only a son survived. He came back, but didn't stay here. You see that building there? That was the storehouse. He'd buy up the rabbit skins from the local men and take them to sell in the city."

I photographed the derelict building hoping that it was not the only tangible memento of pre-war Jewish life I would find.

Soon the news spread on the grapevine that three women who were interested in the past had arrived. A few men and women gathered on the portico of the local museum, an old building that served as a school in the 19th century. They unlocked the door for us to show their remarkable collection of folk costumes, historic photographs and objects ranging from tools to dishes they had gathered through the years. They all spoke Hungarian and were disappointed that we had to drive back to Budapest the same day instead of spending the night in the village.

We listened to the story of the great Palást battle between the armies of Hadim Ali Pasha and Erazmus Teuffel, a battle won by the Turks in 1552 which left thousands of dead scattered in the area. This decisive loss opened the north to Turkish conquest.

History saturates every square mile in Central Europe.

Having been away for many decades in places where people don't seem to carry history in their bone marrow, I felt reinstated in the bloodstained soil of defeats inside the walls of that provincial museum.

After some time spent looking at flags, church and folkloric memorabilia, I asked whether there was anything about Jews left in the area. No, there was not. Although there might be some old men and women who could give information, they said, and somewhere at the very end of the village there once was a Jewish cemetery.

"What about a pub owned by a Jewish family?"

"We haven't heard," said one of the women who invited us for a cup of coffee to her house. Sitting at her table, I answered questions about life in New Zealand. She and her daughter made themselves busy slicing a freshly baked cake and wrapping up slices for us "for the road".

How could I expect anyone to remember in 2005 a pub owner in the 1870s? That was more than six generations back. Pubs changed hands notoriously often.

My two friends were ready to leave, but I insisted upon looking for the old cemetery before it turned dark.

53

Sunken Graves

The road turned sharply to the right, going downhill, and I followed hoping to find some gravesites. My friends, less motivated and consequently getting tired as the day wore on, followed at a distance. I kept going beyond a turn in the road, where the houses thinned out and open land lay ahead, obviously cultivated without a sign of interruptions for burial grounds. I turned back ready to give up, trying to rejoin my friends.

That's when I noticed a small lot to the right, above the roadside ditch, a weed-infested lumpy lot filled with undulating humps and hollows.

"Wait!" I shouted and climbed across the weeds. These humps were manmade and regular. After parting some of the tangled stalks of decades of neglect, I noticed that at each mound's highest point there was a hollow, a low entrance, with a few of them still holding on to the remnants of a wooden door.

I stood there trying to think. An earth hump with a tiny door instantly reminded me of the potato clamps I saw as a child in Püski. They were dug underground, some quite elaborate, and made to last for years to store root vegetables. But nobody there would fill a whole parcel of land with identical clamps.

These humps were built to house families. To bury the dead. I felt sure that I had found the old Jewish cemetery. Yes, it had to be far removed from Christian graves. It had to be unobtrusive without fancy tombstones marked with illegible script to cause confusion and resentment.

This cemetery had survived under the weeds even when nobody was left to weed it.

I climbed down to the road and stopped an old woman walking by leading a dog and asked her if she knew about an old cemetery there.

"No, I don't," she said, "I am new here. I only came after the war 50 years ago."

On the way back to Budapest I didn't feel that my visit was in vain. At the museum a few people exchanged their Email addresses with me and promised to search for the names of Petyán and Sonnenfeld-Szilágyi in the surrounding area.

The only thing I regretted was my reluctance to enter at least one of the humps. Was it because of respect? Or was it because I was afraid to crawl into darkness among swarms of mosquitos and other insects, afraid of what I would find?

Lunch by the Zoo (1930s)

Lunch by the Zoo was a lavish affair
under the shade of trembling trees.
We were pampered by the fine waiters
of Budapest who served us with skill and flourish
Gundel's prize dishes: Crayfish Strudel
Turkey with Goose Liver Stuffed with Chestnuts
washed down with foaming Dreher.

Sitting in cushioned cane armchairs
Mother and Father and assorted friends,
tennis partners and fellow writers in search
of fortune and fame traded gossip and dabbed
their lips with soft damask napkins
between bouts of laughter rippling over my head.

My favourite spot under the table
let me safely survey the restless feet of women
shod in silk stockings and high-heeled cork wedges
cross-legged, tapping the air.
Their men in polished oxfords stretched out straight
presented hurdles as I crawled around
in the tent of the starched tablecloth.

I heard names of people I didn't know:
names like Hitler, Hindenburg and the more musical
Mussolini sounding as sweet as the cream
in the spoon my father handed me when espresso
was served with whipped cream and chocolate *mignons.*
I watched his other hand stroking my mother's knees.

"Why don't you go to the swings?"
she asked. But I hated the swings where kids
much bigger and rougher acted like queens and kings.

It was much safer to crawl under the table
and listen to birds cry in their cages,
hyenas bark, elephants trumpet
and monkeys chatter and howl behind steel bars.

A few years later, in 1944-45,
they were all left to starve
and die of thirst and bullets
just like those around the table
who never came back.

54

Palást keeps its promise

Not long after my return to New Zealand, I received an e-mail from a bright young student of history living in Palást. She had been contacted by one of the curators of the village museum and offered to help me in my search for Ómama's relatives. She promptly dived into all the possible sources she could find in Bratislava and Budapest. Her expertise and diligence was soon rewarded, and she reported to me in another of her e-mails:

> "In the 19th century Miksa Sonnenfeld changed his name to Miksa Szilágyi.

My source is 'Name Changes in Our Century', a collection of names changed with the permission of local authorities and the minister, 1800-1893, Budapest, published by Viktor Hornyánszky in 1895, 253p.

The name change was recorded in the Ministry of Interior.

Miksa Szilágyi rests in Plot 39, in the second row, grave 40. He was born in 1869 and died in 1930. The grave of your grandmother, Gizella Petyán (born 1880, died 1947) is the fifth grave from his in Budapest."

So they were laid to rest only four graves apart from each other.

It was Apu who chose to bury his mother close to his father. In his forties by then, he managed, as much as it was possible, to fulfill a child's desire for a reunion.

55

Words of mouth

In further e-mails sent by the tireless young researcher, the story of the few Jews extant in the village of Palást in the 1940s started to emerge.

A 93-year-old elder recalled three families. She told her that besides the Rosenbergs and Langers, there were the Blumentárs [sic]. They ran a small shop, but moved away before the war.

Everybody liked the Rosenbergs and the Langers, said the old woman. They had shops, worked the land and often helped out the needy with loans. They were taken away on horse-drawn carriages, and nobody dared to ask where they went even if they felt sorry for them. She didn't recall a Petyán family.

But she remembered what old Rosenberg, a family patriarch, said as he turned towards the silently staring bystanders when he was forced to mount a carriage. "Today it is us. Just wait. Tomorrow it will be your turn."

His prediction was recalled by the villagers when it came to a sudden pass after the war, in the years of turmoil and shifting borders. It was the occasion of the forced evacuations of Hungarians who refused to call themselves Slovaks.

56

Petyáns on the list

Another local historian sent me the picture of a Holocaust memorial erected to commemorate the victims in the Ipolyság area. Scanning the names of the taken and killed, I managed to find "Petyán and family". No first names. Just family. Two? Four? Six? More? From where exactly? My inquiries led me nowhere.

I still don't know whether they were close relations, but I am sure now that there were Petyáns in Hont County somewhere around Palást. That's where my Ómama learned to speak fluent Slovakian and to communicate easily with the Russian soldiers billeted with us during the siege of Budapest.

NEMSIC Z. NEMSIC Z.
NEU L. OBLAT SZ. OBLAT I.
A. PASKUS F. PASKUS L.
PETYAN ÉS CS.
POLACSEK I.
POLACSEK M. POLACSEK S.
POLGÁR I. POLGÁR F. POLICER G.
RÉVÉSZ C. RÉVÉSZ L.
ROSENBERG H. ROSENBERG M.
ROSENZWEIG B. ROSENZWEIG

57

A mystery man

Searching for my father's father could be based on a few facts and some certainty. For my mother's any search proved to be futile, no matter how many attempts I had made to track him down.

I had no name. The closest I got to him happened through a few words of Aunt Mari more than half a century after Grandma's death. Nobody else mentioned him. He disappeared before Anyu was born.

The man I learned to call Grandpa by the time I was two I can only picture through the stories Grandma told me when she was in a mellow mood reminiscing about the man she married.

58

Grandpa

Grandma moved to Budapest in search of a better life for herself and for her illegitimate daughter. She not only found work in a factory, but a husband as well, József Palkó, a handsome and hard-working arrival from another village, who married her and adopted her daughter.

When my step-grandpa died I was not yet three. My image of him had nothing to do with knives or chickens. It had to do with horses and fiacres, the elegant black cabs of the past.

Grandma told me about his work. How he used to wait in front of pubs late in the night hoping for customers to stagger out to the street. How he had to lift out of his cab heavy drunks who had fallen asleep by the time he got them home. How he had to carry them to the door, where their wives in their nightgowns stood with hands on their hips. "Sometimes they were so angry, they refused to pay for the cab, as if it was your grandpa's fault."

She told me how he would shiver on his seat in winter and how he would cover his horse with a blanket, while he waited in the icy streets. "He'd come home, empty his pockets, put the money on the table, his fingers stiff and red, the tip of his nose frozen. I had to boil water and give him a hot foot bath to thaw out his feet."

Grandpa had a moustache in my dreams, gloved hands and a bent back under a black coat covered with snow. He carried a small sack of hay and hung it over the ears of a big brown horse that eagerly buried its muzzle in the feed.

"He fell off the seat of his fiacre one day. They brought him home. It was no use. His heart gave up. For a time you kept looking for him. 'Where is Grandpa? Where is he?' But you were small and soon forgot.

"He used to lift you up and let you pat Rigó. And Rigó was patient, didn't move, it let you stroke its ears. But your grandpa didn't let you poke its eyes and never let you sit on its back. Only on the fiacre. You pleaded. You wanted to sit on the horse."

Cockcrow

Another dawn:
a faint smear of white chalk
on the ebony blackboard of the night.
I watch it spread and redraw the world.
Thus dawns the sharpening outline
of my life and of all existence,
a vision more acute every day.

That's why I,
a bungling midwife to each birthing morning,
that's why I stand by to raise the sun.

Stopping to see

A sudden sunbeam collides
with a scuffed red plastic measuring cup
left on the kitchen table.

The ordinary transformed into luminous ruby
glows with the bestowed glory
sent by a burning star.

I eye its brazen brilliance,
its dominance over the varnished table,
over a spoon dim in the shade
stuck into marmalade
in a glass jar.

The time I waste without haste
beguiled by the passing light
I cherish as much as any sight
I may alight upon
on the day
when with halting breath
I'll try to wrest
with all my might
one more, just one more delight.

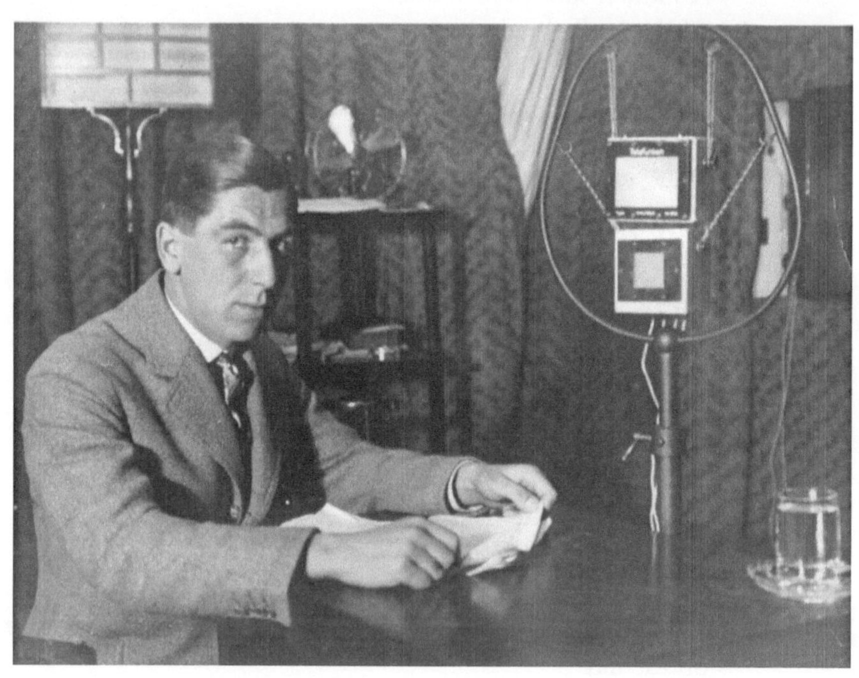

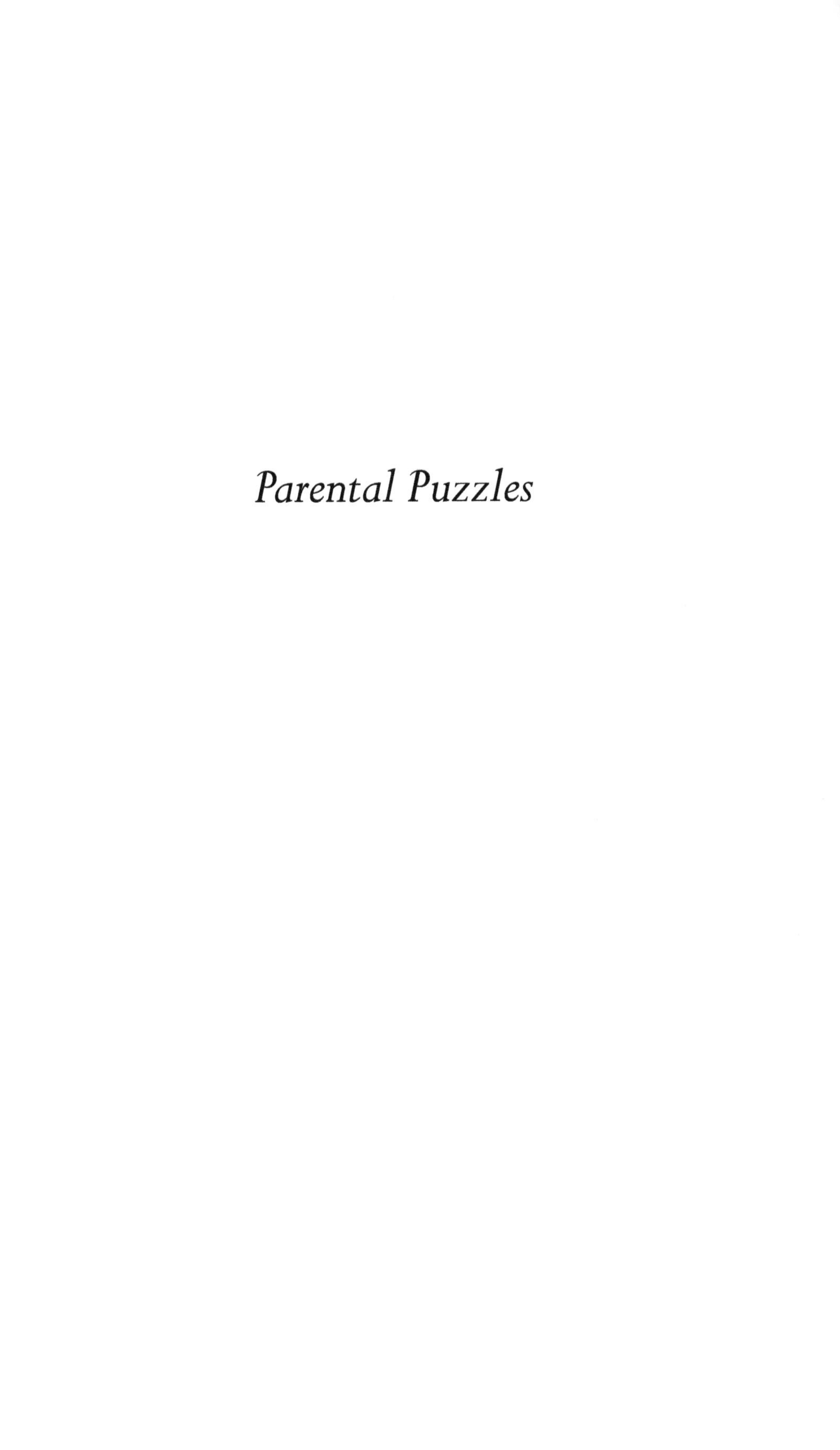

Parental Puzzles

59

Mother's start

When I was older than Anyu when she died, I was back in Püski, the village of her birth and childhood, looking for her footprints.

Where is the house where she lived as a child?

Long gone, washed away in a flood.

Did she have playmates?

She had no time to play.

While I was raking through the memories of village elders and was walking on the narrow lanes where she walked long ago, I could envision her childhood and her determination to rise above years of humiliation.

Yes, her life began in 1902, born as the bastard daughter of a dirt-poor peasant girl in a strictly Roman Catholic village where illegitimacy delivered contempt, where her lot was to take on menial work as a child, looking after animals and helping out in the fields.

A century after her birth, it was Auntie Mari - a fragile bundle of bones in her 99th year whom I encountered curled up like a shrimp on a bench in front of her house - who told me about Anyu's blood father, the man who got away.

"People said that he was a good-lookin' man, older than your grandma was. A big manager of the big estate where she worked. He sent her some money after your mother was born. Yes, by that time he had quit and moved. No, nobody knew where he went. Just buggered off.

"But he was decent enough to pay something at least. Not much. Never came back. No, I don't know his name."

Auntie Mari, not a blood relative, was related to us through her marriage to one of Grandma's nephews. I visited her as a child in her house on New Row in Püski many times. A house I got to know in great detail including the slant of the dirt floor and the coats hanging on nails by the door waiting to be mended. There was a smell of dampness and the buzz of regiments of flies.

This poem is about two of my visits, one as a child, the other much later:

Auntie Mari
(1880–1979)

She had no children.
By the time I was born she was so old,
everybody called her Auntie Mari
even elderly shopkeepers
and the village priest who drank too much
of Christ's blood from the church chalice.

I spent summer hours in Auntie's kitchen
munching ripe pears and
watching flies buzz trying to get out

of her glass fly catcher
already filled with the floating corpses
of yesterday's flies.

She stayed in her bed,
snug under a goose feather comforter
in the semi-dark room
where I was sent to pay a visit,
an awkward city child,
facing a village matriarch.

She motioned me to lean closer,
reached under her pillow
with a hand wrinkled and gnarled
by labour in sun and snow,
pulled out a handful of
freshly shelled walnuts
with a wink and a smile,
and I was obliged to eat
while she stared.

They said
she had buried two husbands.
The third was a tailor
who sewed men's trousers
and made-to-measure coats.
He lost a leg in the war,
never spoke, but kept her well off
getting paid in eggs and lard
wheat and rye, barley,
husked corn for the pigs.

She asked me to chase the flies out of her room.
I closed the door and went back to sit at the table
to watch death enacted over and over
in the fly trap
by a frantic hum of wings.

She lived to ninety-nine,
buried the third one,
not to mention great-nephews, nieces,
emperors, kings, presidents,
dictators, liberators, and thousands of
generations of flies under the glass dome.

I was a grown wife when I last saw her.
She was sitting on a bench

outside her mud house.
Aunt Mari,
shriveled, shrimp-like,
light as a feather,
rose to embrace me and when she heard
that my husband was a bearded Englishman
she laughed.
"Wonderful," she said.
"Then he tickles."

60

Anyu the flapper

Grandma was ambitious for her clever daughter. She decided to put her into a good commercial high school. She could earn some money to pay for her books by sewing and washing the laundry of the rich, who were numerous in the big city.

Her teachers insisted that she let the bright girl, top of her class, go on studying. One of them went as far as visiting them, begging to let her carry on, but necessity ruled and she was obliged to quit and go to work.

By her early teens, she was a skilled typist and faultless speller. She learned to transform into shorthand hurried dictations no matter how fast, and could mentally edit into perfectly flowing prose the confused words of a boss. She became familiar with legal matters by working as a secretary for a lawyer.

She was not yet 20 when Apu noticed her. She was lively, dressed well and proved to be a challenge. My father, young and eager to get on in the world, was already working for newspapers since he was 16.

I am sure that Anyu was impressed by his attentions. 'Upwardly mobile' through her intelligence, she was hungry for new adventures at Apu's side: travel, tennis, literary glories, the stimulating company of actors, writers, filmmakers, characters remote from her village childhood and the constricted horizon of her adolescence.

Lacrimae Rerum

The rounding off meted out by death
car crash, cancer, hurricanes
the charnel-house of chance
make life stories easier to write.
Finality flashes meaning on the screen.

Still,
How could I dare to judge
the dead I loved,
to dig up bones
buried under pieties and lies?

To decipher blotched letters
written when smitten by desire
they swore eternal love
ending in betrayal?

Do I dare to scatter the dust
of pressed flowers saved in a box
under dog-eared photos of infants
long laid to rest in neglected graves?

Who wants to sink a knife
into his own flesh and gut
to lay bare the truth
nothing but?

61

Father's darlings…

My mother had kept the passionate postcards father sent her, some dating back as far as the early 1920s, neatly glued into the album I inherited.

Father could not bring himself to throw them away after she died, but kept them hidden from his second wife in a bundle tucked into the bottom of a drawer in his office desk. After he died, my stepmother, in turn, decently packed them up, together with his rings, best shirts and cufflinks, and posted them to New Zealand.

At first, I also hid the bundle in a box I kept in the back of a shelf because I could not bear to read this flotsam of love long lost and buried. Now, almost a century later, I can read his lines calmly.

> My dear darling! Do you remember this sailing dinghy? It floated by us on the mirror smooth water of Balaton. I cut down this picture to the size of a postcard and will send it to you with many kisses. Your Laci

Laci is a pet name for László.

Another:

> My darling! At the moment it is Saturday 1:30 pm and I am attending an auto show. If there is such a thing as auto-suggestion (apropos of the many autos surrounding me), then at this very moment you must also think about me. Because I am thinking about you, my dear little girl. Can you see it clearly on my face in this photo? Your loving Laci

This was written in 1926, seven years before my birth.

In later missives when he moved to Berlin, he wrote about the unheated antique shop where he lay shivering with fever. He wrote that he needed to get out of there and rent a room, he knew a place, but he had no money.

Money management, sending relief sums from Budapest was an important role of the young typist.

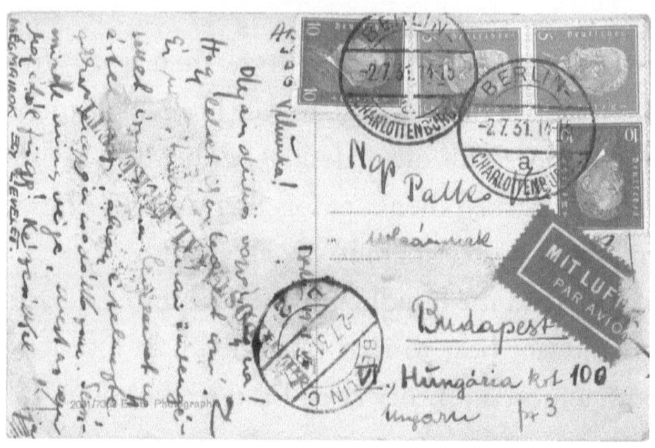

> My dearest darling! Engel will call on you on Wednesday. You must give him ten pengős. My lovely, can you come to me in Berlin? Kisses, kisses, yours forever.

My future mother promptly settled the sum that he had borrowed from Engel.

And there is a postcard addressed to the office where she worked on Hungária Road. His words of protestation suggest that she had her moments of doubt, moments of wanting out. What she wrote to him is lost. He did not save it.

Here is his indignant response full of exclamation marks, scrawled hurriedly on the back of a photograph of Pariser Platz with

Branderburger Tor, sent off urgently by air mail, not by slow train like the rest:

> Darling! I am furious! How could you write a letter like that? I am not capable of writing 'gushing effusions', and I am amazed if you interpret my letters that way. Nothing is over between us, it can't be because that doesn't depend on you!

On whom did it depend?

He was right. It was not over, in spite of my mother's unerring intuition. Or was it premonition?

Thinking back, I assume that his effusive style may have developed as a matter of survival at first, the style of a son whose father had walked out. It could grow out of a need and an early insecurity and gradually became part of his nature. He turned into a gushing lover, a gushing husband, a gushing father.

After Olga, his second wife also died, I inherited the rhapsodic poems he wrote for her birthdays for many decades, starting while I was still a small child. His love poems addressed to her used the same endearments I had heard him use to please my mother.

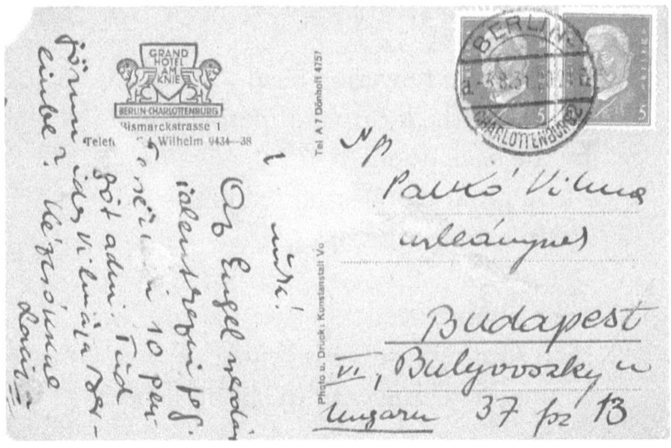
GRAND HOTEL AM KNIE
BERLIN-CHARLOTTENBURG
Bismarckstrasse 1
Telefon: Wilhelm 9434—38

Palkó Vilma
urleány
Budapest
VI, Bulyovszky u.
37 fsz 13

My old friend, a Santa Barbara psychiatrist, who knew my father when we were children, told me that he probably loved my mother just the same, that it is possible to love two women at once. "She probably knew all along," she said. "Most women did. But that generation of women didn't want to know that they knew. They put it in the back of their mind and carried on. Divorce was out of the question."

Now I know that his out-of-town assignments, when he stayed away "working" for days, were often spent beside Lake Balaton or in the mountains with his lover. When he returned with small treats for me and gifts to delight my mother, I always ran to him.

"Apu! What did you bring me?"

"Apu, tell me how was your trip?"

Impatience

"The insect does not aim at so much glory.
It confines itself showing us life in the
inexhaustible variety of its manifestations,
it helps us decipher in some small measure
the obscurest book of all, the book of ourselves."
(Jean- Henri Fabre, Mintaurus typhoeus)

They raise a flowering head
above the thick carpet of periwinkle
by the back door.
Neon pink, blood-drop red petals
strain towards the sun.

Such abundance,
such seeding lust is irresistible
to the furry hunger of the bumble bee.
Its weight bends the stem

as it burrows head first
to suck the sweet centre,
triumphant offering
in the name of fecundity.

Beauty and beast,
two unsheathed wills meet
in the foraging frenzy of beating wings.
The bee takes what's on offer
by the equal thirst of brazen petals.

62

Anyu's last card

A week before she died in 1958, my mother wrote to me. It was different from all the postcards she sent me from her hospital bed where she was bedbound for six months due to a blood clot in her leg after a hysterectomy.

*

The words before were written in ink, and I knew that the ink came from my father's Montblanc, that he was sitting on the edge of her hospital bed, addressed the card and handed it to her to finish and sign. They had written together all the earlier ones, Anyu's pearly letters highly legible, Apu's hurriedly scrawled. Her short missives were unfailingly optimistic and referred only to the immediate present. "I am feeling much stronger. The doctor let me get up this morning. I sat by the window on a chair for an hour. The trees are shedding their leaves in the wind…"

For this last note she used a pencil, not Apu's fountain pen. He was not there. She wrote it alone. The pressure of graphite made indentations in the paper, as if she had intended to carve an emphatic summary even the blind could read. She engraved every word.

> "Panni!
> Yes, I have come a long way from the barefoot girl in the village herding flocks of geese for our neighbours who were better off…"

Her words made me think that she was attempting to sum up her life while she was forced to lie on a hospital bed for months on end. It was an assertive post card. It was meant for me, just for me, not for Apu or anyone else. It was meant to convey the road she had taken on the way to becoming my mother, the wife of a writer in cosmopolitan Budapest. A story I might forget living in a faraway land across the sea.

It was never mailed. I received it decades later stuck among old photos and documents. For a while I kept it on my desk to read and re-read it and copied the first sentence into my notebook, then I put it away in a safe place. So safe that I cannot find it no matter how thoroughly I search through drawers, envelopes and derelict shoeboxes filled with hundreds of old photos and rolls of undeveloped film sent from Budapest. Olga did her duty, a sign of her devotion to my father, the man who was her lover before my mother passed away clearing the way for their marriage.

Photographs seem to have an afterlife when they become forensic evidence. After Olga's death, her stash of mementos also landed in New Zealand by courtesy of the people who dismantled and occupied her room.

Pictures of clandestine trips to mountain retreats lay open in neatly annotated albums on my kitchen table. I could read the poems Apu wrote to celebrate her birthdays and their reconciliations after lovingly detailed quarrels.

To this day I wonder how many years did my mother hide her existence from me and then kept writing with my father those happy joint postcards addressed to Maine, to New York and Florida, Ohio and California, imagined places she never reached.

An old friend of mine in Budapest told me close to 50 years after my mother's death that after my departure she often went to visit her mother. She arrived crying and kept asking whether she should stay put or seek a divorce.

In 2014 I wrote the following poem:

I'll bring home

(Dedicated to my mother who died in 1958)

I will bring home all the streets
wide and narrow,
streets I walked on five continents.

I'll sing you the old songs
about sailing into sunsets
about love won and lost,
melodies we used to hum
way back then, when
we gathered around radios,

I'll bring the photos I shot
of people you never met:
fractured airport farewells,
weepy weddings, naked newborns,
funerals in winter storms.

I'll tell you tales true and untrue
but good to hear and have a laugh,
tales of bungles and triumphs.

I'll sit down at our table
watch your blue eyes focus
spellbound on my moving lips.

And your eyes will shine again
from the same baffled face
I left countless years ago
in the house, long demolished,
at the table I abandoned
and left too late to reset
for our grand
prodigal reunion.

63

My father's zigzag years

Calamity shadowed Apu's childhood.

I can only speculate how he felt when his father left the household and moved in with another woman. The children stayed with Ómama.

At the time of the divorce, he was somewhere under ten years old.

Soon he had to cope with the sudden deaths of his older brother and sister, both victims of diseases without comprehension or cure at the time.

In the turmoil of his adolescence, he turned his back on religious conventions. He concentrated on school and helping out at home.

64

A determined boy

Growing up alone with her mother, who kept trying various ways to make a living, was not easy. She depended on her only remaining son.

He told me about some of his duties.

"When Ómama opened a greengrocer shop in Terézváros, I had to deliver potatoes, onions, bunches of parsley, pumpkins and so on, also fruit in season to customers in the neighbourhood. Mother would get up in the dark, pack up the orders and I would lug them up the stairs in the tenements, pocket the change and bring it to her. I did this early in the morning, before school.

"When she found that she could sell the aprons she wore in the shop, she started sewing them in the evening, and I'd take the ready aprons to shops to sell. Bakers and butchers especially loved her strong aprons. She got some more women who needed money sewing these aprons in their home, and I picked them up when they were ready and paid for them.

"Then my mother rented a big old house not far from the Zoo and we moved in there. She kept one room for us and transformed the rest into a boarding house. Zoo workers and circus performers rented the rooms. The circus tent used to be near the Zoo, and we had the most interesting tenants sitting around the breakfast table. There were clowns, lion tamers, dressage riders, sword swallowers, fire-eaters and acrobats. All of them were kind to me, and let me in their shows for free. But a few of them drank a lot, and one of them committed suicide in his room. Mother did all the cooking, and I helped with the cleaning after school. I learned juggling and for a while I wanted to be a tightrope walker."

School became for him a place to rest.

Ómama wanted Apu to be educated and get ahead, and so did he. A Reál Gimnázium was their choice with its practical curriculum. He made many lifelong friends among his classmates and also managed to make some pocket money by starting a handmade chess magazine he could sell. Chess remained his passion that he tried to pass on to me without much success.

What did he do with the pocket money? He bought a second-hand tennis racket and started to hang out around the tennis court by the Zoo. A ball boy at first, eager and polite, soon he was invited to step in for a missing fourth.

But his main ambition remained writing, which meant journalism. He kept trying and was sent packing by various editors, until he penned a report of a house fire he accidentally stumbled upon in the neighborhood. He earned his first byline, and seeing his name in print in a daily paper hooked him for life.

"I was also attracted to the theatre, acted in school, wanted to see every play, to talk to actors and I wanted to be a playwright," he told me.

He dreamed of working for *Theatre Life*.

A teenager? He answered me:

> As a joke, the editor trying to get rid of me, told me: 'Bring me a brilliant interview with the most famous actress in Budapest.'
>
> I went to the National Theatre and sneaked in the back door with a large bunch of actors pretending to be one of them. I waited until the end of the show and stationed myself near the dressing rooms. When someone asked me what I was doing there, I said, 'I have to deliver something to Bajor Gizi.' They left me alone. She rushed by me and slammed the door behind herself. I waited for a while, until I managed to gather my courage to knock.
>
> 'Who is it?'

I shouted that I was a delivery man. All I had in my hand was the latest issue of *Theatre Life.*

'Come in,' she said. She was seated in front of a mirror removing her makeup. Such a beautiful woman. I stuttered. This is the magazine, I said, and I promised the editor there that I'll interview you.

She laughed. 'You are a schoolboy. How old are you?'

'Seventeen,' I lied.

She laughed again, 'Then hurry up. I am due to meet someone in ten minutes.'

She got up and stepped behind a screen. 'Get going!' she said, and started to undress, with her costume landing on the top of the screen. I was speechless. 'Hand me the coat that hangs on the door.' I turned and lifted a fur coat over the screen. She stepped out, buttoned the fur coat and sat down again to arrange her hair, smiling at me through the mirror. 'The cat got your tongue,' she said. 'What kind of a reporter are you?'

That got me going. I asked her all kinds of questions that suddenly came to mind; why did she choose acting, why does she like doing it, what does she think of her audience, is she happy with every role, which play she likes the most, which play she would like to be in next, and so on. She answered all of my questions by the time there was a knock on the door and a man in a camelhair coat entered. I don't know who he was. I left in a daze. But in the next issue of the magazine I had my story headlined on the cover, and I was hired. That's how I became a journalist.

65

A happy raconteur

My father could tell more stories and jokes than anyone else I knew. He managed to meet, to interview, to track down the famous, the unknown, those on the way up and those who were about to die and could talk to him bluntly because they had nothing to lose any more by telling the truth.

A few years before he died in 1979, he was writing an unfinished memoir about his career. Reading the crumbling pages, one gets the impression that he knew everybody who mattered in politics, literature, music, the theatre and in the criminal courts from the 1920s to the 1970s and that he felt he had a lucky life in exciting times.

One could be tempted to accuse him of mere name dropping, if his quick hops from name to name were not backed up by the anecdotes he told and the short stories that later emerged from some of his encounters. He simply shared the infatuation of his age with celebrity, a trait that is still dominant today. He let people reveal themselves with their own words, and the result often was far from adulation.

The following excerpt, roughly translated by me, is typical of his memory's reliance on anecdotes he told and retold around the tribal tables of Budapest coffeehouses.

Apu's words:

"In the time of Brüning in Berlin I met with many world-famous intellectuals. I interviewed Albert Einstein, Thomas Mann, Franz Lehár, Heinrich Mann and Erich Maria Remarque as well.

"The writer, who became famous with *"All Quiet on the Western Front" (Im Westen nichts Neues)* died in September 1970. He was still a young man when I met him… in the Augsburger Strasse bar called 'Lili' in Berlin and asked him for an interview… He agreed and told me about his early years without hesitation.

"He said that he started at the weekly *Sport im Bild* and that he also wrote a book about the methods of cocktail mixing.

"When he finished *"All Quiet on the Western Front"* and took it to Ullstein publishers, he was told that nobody would be interested in a book about a war after a defeat. A little later, however, they realized the possibility of profit, he said. Before they started printing, they bought up all extant copies of the cocktail book, not wanting the bestseller and a "how to" book on the market simultaneously.

'How many copies have been printed?' I asked.

"'Up till now about 15 million copies. I became a rich man, bought a house in Ascona and started to collect French impressionists.'

"But Europe didn't stay silent long in the calendar year of 1932.

"When a few days later I took the Remarque interview to the German paper *12 Uhr Blatt,* they accepted it, and the film editor told me that the famous writer had not been totally frank with me. He kept quiet about his true name, Erich Remark, and about another book, *'Die Traumbunde',* written under his old name, published by Schönheit Verlag in Dresden. Remarque felt embarrassed by this erotic book about bohemian artists. When Schönheit Verlag started to advertise that they had published an earlier novel by the writer of *'All Quiet in the Western Front',* Remarque ordered a stop to the advertising campaign.

"He did not need *Die Traumbunde* in his CV any more."

The times my father most liked to remember were his twenties and early thirties, the period before political realities scuttled his ambitions. Those were the years when he started publishing his murder mysteries, adventure stories in instalments and his pulp paperbacks. That was when he started working for *Borsszem Jankó*, a venerable satirical paper, honing his sense of humour which was used in his later years at another humorous weekly, the *Ludas Matyi*.

66

Apu's best friend

In his unfinished memoir, my father named Andor Zsoldos as his best friend. He was ten years older than Apu, who always seemed to treat him with deference. Zsoldos himself had shown no deference towards anyone; he commanded attention and gave the impression of a haughty intellectual in a hurry to attend to important matters.

Apu thought him brilliant. He met him in Berlin in the 1920s, a callow youth then himself, and later asked him and his wife to be the witnesses at his wedding.

At the time Zsoldos arrived in Berlin he was already thirty and he had worked as an actor, a journalist, playwright and director in Hungary and gained experience in the film industry in Paris and Nice.

He threw himself into the creative whirlwind of Berlin as a writer-producer-director rolled into one and, among others, he collaborated with Max Reinhardt. His filmography lists 14 titles.

One of Apu's often repeated and "never fail" coffeehouse anecdotes was about Zsoldos trying to convince a German meat-millionaire to back one of the films for which he wrote the screenplay.

I was not surprised to find this story included in my father's autobiography. I include it here as well, because it throws light on the general hustling atmosphere of Weimar era bohemian life, which nonetheless generated various masterpieces that are still fodder to imitators today.

My father's words are translated from Hungarian:

"My best friend in Berlin was Andor Zsoldos who was previously on the editorial staff of *Nap* and *Szinházi Élet*. He was also a fine poet who neglected poetry in favour of motion pictures. He fulfilled three roles in Berlin; he was the producer and director of the Melodie film company and he wrote and directed several films. One of his great successes was a film about Dreyfus.

In Berlin it was necessary to find backers for films. Rich merchants and industrialists were glad to finance films promising big profits. Somebody introduced Zsoldos to a rich meat producer not very well versed in literature. He instantly liked the Dreyfus story about a French cavalry officer wrongly charged with treason.

"Who wrote this?" he asked.

"Emile Zola," said Zsoldos, "but I adapted it to film."

"All right. You get the money, but only if this Emil will come along to watch the production. Tell him."

"That will be difficult. That's because ...the writer...well...he is in Paris."

"I take no risks. What if he doesn't like your script? He can stop the filming. I'll pay for your trip to Paris to bring him with you."

"That would be all right, but I am pretty sure that Zola will refuse to come."

"Then there'll be no film."

"I have a brilliant proposition that might work for us," said Zsoldos with great enthusiasm. He could never speak any other way, only in superlatives. "I'll go there and I'll read to him the whole script, and if he has no objections, then we can go ahead and the cameras can start to roll."

"All right," agreed the millionaire, "get going tomorrow."

"I'll go today."

Zsoldos travelled to Paris and upon arrival proceeded to Émile Zola's crypt in the Panthéon, opened his filmscript of the Dreyfus affair and read it aloud from start to finish.

The next day he came back to Berlin and told the meat man the truth; Zola had not objected to a single word. The filming could start.

Later basking in the great success of the film, the millionaire said to Zsoldos, "It's a pity. This writer at least should've turned up at the premier."

67

Chop suey with Zsoldos

Hitler changed Berlin. Artists scattered to the four corners of the world. My parents and the Zsoldos family returned to Budapest to no avail because Hitler's men soon followed them.

I was born in October, and Apu managed to grab his camera and take a photo of the two Zsoldos children pushing me around in a baby carriage. The daughter, now a psychiatrist in California, remembers our family visits to their home.

My memory starts with eating cream and custard in coffee houses with Zsoldos and his wife, a vivacious and elegant woman.

The conversation was about things that I was too young to care about.

It was always Zsoldos who spoke the most and, if his wife tried to enter the conversation, he would turn to her as soon as she said a few words and tell her to shut up. She would look hurt and I would feel uncomfortable not daring to look at either of them.

My parents seemed to take this in their stride, and the talk would resume mostly between the two men, exchanging anecdotes, jokes and gossip about people I didn't know. Anyu would quietly sip her coffee for a while, then turn and start to chat about films or books with Mrs Zsoldos, who never complained.

Much later her daughter told me that whenever she and her brother arrived home from school, they were scared to go inside and find their father in a bad mood. Men of that generation were often despots in the home who ruled by ruthless humiliation.

Their family moved to Vienna and America later, and I lost contact with my father's best friend for years.

After 1956, when I was still a new and naive refugee in America living in San Francisco, I received a surprise phone call one day. It was Zsoldos who wanted to meet me. I told him that I could not invite him to my rented room. No guests were allowed to enter, according to the house rules. He invited me to dinner in Chinatown.

This was my first visit to Chinatown, a magic place at night that I would not consider then entering alone. The densely crowded streets, shop windows crammed with glittering porcelain knick-knacks, vendors dressed in brilliant silks adding up their bills on abacuses, restaurants booming with diners at ten at night, the whole scene seemed to me a sweeping oriental carnival. Hearing Chinese all around was like landing on a new planet.

Zsoldos, white-haired and elegant in the way of a 1920s gentleman with the perfect triangle of a white handkerchief sticking out of his breast pocket, also seemed to be from another world.

He was attentive and generous, wanting to know all the details of my life and, as he escorted me home, he emphatically ordered me to move out of my rented room, where I was not allowed to entertain guests, and to get a decent apartment suitable for a healthy sex life.

The next time I saw him was in Ventura, after my son was born, and he came to deliver a formal blessing over his crib.

"For his protection," he said.

68

Apu's Kodak

Neither of my grandmothers, not Grandma nor Ómama, ever had a camera. Father, always keen on the latest technology, had the first Kodak in the family, and when he was courting my mother, he took a photo of his future mother-in-law, Grandma and her husband.

I have inherited this one small photo of Grandma in her 40s. No other picture remains from her younger years.

She is sitting in the paved yard of a house next to her decent, upright husband. The grainy black and white, shot in the 1920s, is the only photo I have of them together.

Grandma is not in the forefront, she is sitting with Gyuri dog on her lap behind two men playing cards. Her husband, Palkó József sits on a low *sámli,* cards in hand, pipe in mouth, dark trousers, clean white shirt, with the air of a contented *pater familias.* In front of him is a *hokedli* commandeered from the kitchen to act as a table. It must have been Sunday. And summer.

Across from him sits a mysterious stranger. There is no identification scrawled on the back of the picture. He is a tall, handsome young man perching on a four-legged stool, wearing a similarly pristine white shirt and looking very much like a film star, a possible heartthrob, who is definitely not my father. Could he be a forester? Standing in the background, withdrawn into the semi-darkness of an open door is a young woman with her head cut off by the camera.

Why am I sure that this headless woman is my mother in hesitant withdrawal from the dominant scene? Does it have to do with the contentment in the faces of Grandma and József and with the ease of the young man in their company?

Is he the ideally attractive and well-positioned young forester Grandma talked about, who pursued my mother assiduously and not only was in love "head over heels", but could have assured her a secure and comfortable place in society "in these perilous times"?

I tend to think that this grainy old photo (Was it shot and developed by my father who chanced to call upon his sweetheart unexpectedly and provided additional reason for mother to stay out of the picture?) suggests two distinct possibilities for my own set of genes.

Apu and his cameras continued on their triumphant tour of the city, capturing its streets, its dinner parties, its characters both famous and odd.

Judging by my stack of old negatives, at first he focused on my future mother. He made her pose against rocks, arms raised, snapping her purse shut, or sitting by the Danube staring at the waves, crossing her legs, her chin resting on the back of her hand, throwing a smile towards her man.

Those were heady days.

Graduating from Kodak to Rolleiflex after 1929, cameras remained an inseparable part of Apu's personality.

A tattered photo shows him holding one close to his chest while he is perched on a high fence in the zoo.

On another one he is grinning while standing on the top of a wagon packed with demijohns idling in a railroad station, ready to snap something newsworthy among a gathering of motley men ranging from important burghers in hats and coats to railroad men in pseudo-military uniforms and working-class men in shabby work clothes.

When the occasion called for it, he would rent tails and a top hat and stand in the privileged spot of a bona fide press photographer in front of a crowd gathered for a momentous event that no one is left alive to identify.

Another photo shows him on a rooftop facing a misty city (Berlin? Budapest? Vienna? Pozsony? Prague?) with his camera aiming at the sky.

My childhood was haunted by the ubiquitous "Rollei", and after many a "stand here", "move over there", "give me a smile", instructions, I learned to pose and grin.

It is noticeable though that after a while the focus shifts from woman to child, and in later years my mother alone rarely appears. That is why I like to contemplate a small photo where she stands without me in another capacity, as a smiling professional among her colleagues at the financial firm, Büchler Zsigmond & Társa, where she is an equal with the bosses of the firm, the only woman surrounded by respectable desk-bound men under the trees of Szabadság Square (What was its name then?) next to the soon to be closed Budapest Stock Exchange.

IZE

69

Foresters carry poisonous flowers

When I first heard about the "staunch forester" from Grandma, I imagined a tall, beefy man in muddy leather boots and a loose shirt with his sleeves rolled up and a knife stuck in his belt. Or maybe a leaner man, more like the forester in *Snow White and the Seven Dwarfs*, getting ready to kill.

She was rapidly slicing onions and mincing parsley without looking at me, the big knife moving in a steady rhythm.

This time her voice had a thread of iron.

"Of course, your mother could have married Imre and lived in a sturdy wood house of her own in the middle of a forest right by the Danube. Regular pay, free firewood. She wouldn't ever have to go to work. She could be at home, raising you in comfort."

"Who's Imre?" I asked.

"The forester. You should've seen him stand under the window at the hospital where your mother was quarantined and almost died. Scarlet fever. She had it bad. He came with flowers, but nobody was allowed to go in. So he stood under the window trying to see her, but couldn't. He had to give the flowers to a nurse."

"Where is he?"

"Back in the forest. By the Danube. I'm telling you, he was crazy about your mother. But she…"

"What happened?"

"She recovered and came home all right."

"And Imre?"

"Imre was a famous hunter. But your mother liked tennis better. She decided to play tennis with your father instead."

I knew all about Snow White, so forests and knives scared me. I was glad that Anyu chose tennis.

Cabbage Song

When I was terrified
of standing up
in front of a class
back in first grade
my father told me
to look straight ahead
and to see each head
as a cabbage.

It worked.
My speech went
without a hitch
and reaped the reward
of a medal hung on a ribbon
pinned to my chest.

Ever since then
when I see a cabbage
I have the urge
to stand and orate
passionate speeches
sermons that threaten
to raise the dead

because it
never does
smirk or giggle
fidget or fiddle
just sits calmly
and nods its big head
the best audience to be had.

70

Annyi baj legyen!

"Annyi baj legyen!"

This sentence, almost a slogan, has become our family motto.

It is impossible to translate it in three words. "Let's have only that many troubles!" makes little sense. What Apu meant when he was saying it over and over was closer to: "Don't worry. If that is all, it's a trifle, it is no trouble at all."

Because in our collective life major and minor setbacks happened regularly, it was his way of stepping over them, forever upholding the possibility that things could get much worse and asserting that as long as we managed to stay alive, there was a way to overcome anything.

Let's say that I had dropped a glass that shattered on the stone floor of the kitchen. "All right, don't cry," Anyu would say and reach for the broom to help me sweep up the shards.

Grandma would shake her head and say, "Don't step on it. Go away!" and I would feel her disapproval of my clumsiness.

Apu would shout the three magic words from the safety of the room, because he almost never entered the kitchen. "Annyi baj legyen!" His words gave me permission to be free of guilt. I could sigh with relief and go back to the room to sit down beside him.

When there was not enough money and he couldn't find buyers for his latest books, when someone important or powerful was rude to him, he would open his palms and look up with a smile, "Annyi baj legyen".

A defiant motto, a mantra, a prayer.

Years later these three words popped up in New York on the day when a smiling man sitting behind his fancy desk in his formal office under the portrait of Joseph Pulitzer at the Columbia School of Journalism told me that my English was not good enough to become a journalist. "I advise you to choose a career in fashion," he said. "There your accent wouldn't matter. It even could be an asset."

As I walked away and descended the steps of the impressive school founded by Pulitzer, another immigrant with a Hungarian accent, I felt angry and humiliated.

I swore that I'd show him, that smiling man. Yes, I'll show him! And by the time I was back in Johnson Hall in my dorm room, I said it aloud, "Annyi baj legyen!"

71

King of the Toothpicks or Fogpiszkáló Király

"My daughter will marry a Toothpick King when she grows up," said Apu to Aunt Janka, who was formidable behind the counter.

I think that's where I heard him say this for the first time, in Aunt Janka's tiny tobacco shop, where the stamps were displayed behind glass on the counter partly blocked from my view by boxes of pipe tobacco and cigarettes. Stacks of postcards with scalloped edges depicting churches and castles were lined up on a rack, tempting me to run my fingers over them to feel their tiny paper teeth. My furtive act, however stealthy, made Aunt Janka say firmly but kindly every time: "Please, don't touch."

The Toothpick King loomed in my imagination like an enormous stick insect, skinny with long, angular limbs and a nodding head covered by a gold crown encrusted with diamonds bigger than the buttons on my coat.

It seemed that the city was dotted with my father's aunties, and they were all short and round with big bosoms resting on the top of counters brimming with desirable objects. Their dimpled elbows framed their breasts as their smiles welcomed us into their shops. Apu and I regularly made the rounds through their doors that activated bells sounding a cheerful ring when we entered and left. I usually ended up with a piece of candy or a couple of *fillérs* in my hands and was told to save the money for a rainy day unless I wanted to buy a chocolate cow, my favourite, right then and there.

I never asked where the Toothpick King lived, just as I never asked about the home of the Easter Rabbit. Still, somehow I sensed that all magical creatures lived somewhere in America, a faraway adventure land, where everything was possible, where money grew on trees and everyone was king. People around me talked about its 'oil

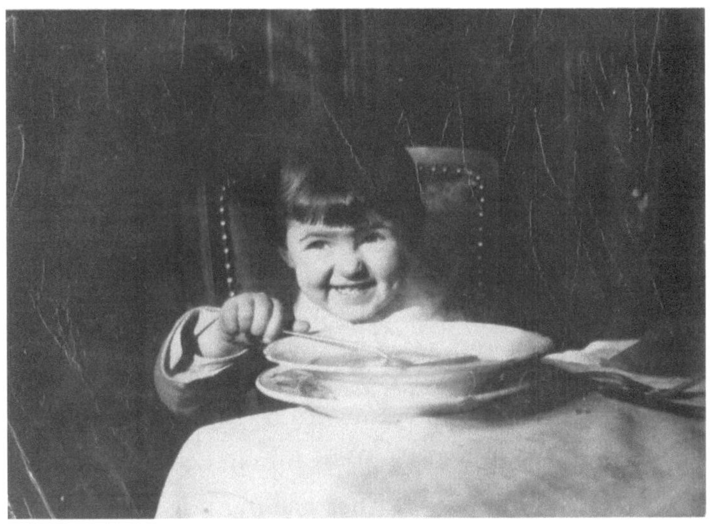

barons', 'movie stars', 'banking giants' and 'railroad tycoons' giving the impression that every industry had its superhuman crowned head in need of a queen like me to complete a state of all-embracing bliss.

I missed Aunt Janka after the war. She was one of those 'who never came back'.

72

My father's rages

Mornings were mostly safe. Apu was the last one to get up. I was already dressed for school, and Anyu had left for work. Grandma would be polishing an apple, buttering bread or slicing smoked bacon in the kitchen for my *tízórai* (morning snack) before Apu would put down the book he was reading and roll out of bed.

Sometimes he kept on reading, or started writing with his head resting against stacked-up pillows while Pipsi would be dozing on his shoulder with its beak tucked into a wing. A notebook rested against his knees, and his Montblanc quickly scurried from left to right across the paper. His flannel pyjamas were dotted with unsightly spots of ink. Grandma often grumbled about them because she had to scrub and scrub to make them disappear.

He considered his writing a sacred ritual requiring total silence. Whispers were deemed even more irritating than normal conversation, not to mention noisily gulping down my breakfast *kakaó* or, even worse, chewing my bread and jam with my mouth open.

During school holidays I might see him in bed until ten or eleven o'clock. Once, when he was neither reading nor writing, just lying still, facing the wall, a pillow stuck over his head, I asked him if he was all right. He sat up and snapped, "Don't interrupt!"

"Oh?"

"I need peace to think. I am working on the plot for the next one."

There was always a next book.

When he had dressed and left, Grandma would comment that this was his standard excuse for being bone-lazy.

I considered both explanations for a while and found myself favouring each depending on my mood, but I never asked him again.

It was not easy to tiptoe around him in our small one-room apartment. On sunny days, I could escape outside and lean over the rail of the *gang*, studying the world. I watched the tired horses patiently standing while their burden of wool bales was unloaded. They were content munching on hay, their nose buried in the burlap sack the drivers hung over their neck, their tail flicking to swat the flies settling on their hide. I kept an eye on the workers in blue overalls pushing carts loaded with the heavy bales towards the back of the factory, while

the office staff dashed around empty-handed in white coats. Their sleeves were protected from ink stains by black cotton covers that were held in place with elastic above their elbows and around their wrists.

I took note of Mr Kelemen, forever hovering around the gate in his official dark blue uniform and, if I timed my inspection right, I could glimpse the postman arriving with bundles of envelopes from the outside world.

I felt that I was unseen and firmly planted as I stood by the rail above the buzz, a spectator in my private theatre filled with action and an established order. The protective cave of our flat was close behind my back. I had everything there: my bed, my own pillow, my dolls and teddy bear. I had my books, my dresses ironed and socks mended by Grandma, my shirts and handkerchiefs kept in meticulous order in our shiny wardrobe.

And there was Grandma to feed me, Apu to make me laugh and Anyu who hugged me when she came home from the office.

On rainy days I stayed inside and read or did my homework while I listened to the clatter of dishes issuing from the kitchen.

Dish clatter could lead to one of Apu's rages.

"Goddam it!" He would shout so loud, he would make me hold my breath. "Why don't you close that damned door, if you must bang the pots."

To which Grandma would respond by slamming two doors shut and resuming a somewhat subdued rattling. Apu would get up with a sigh and disappear into the bathroom.

The most frightening outbursts, however, happened at dinner.

Sunday mornings were wrapped in the smells wafting from every kitchen. Walking home from church, passing under open windows, I could inhale the scent of baking buns, frying onions, the subdued smells of boiling milk, steaming sausages and spicy meatloaves. I could hear the cheery sounds of tables being set, the ringing glasses, the ding of spoons and knives bumping against each other.

Above this melody, in counterpoint were the voices of women, hurried but assured, of children, shrill and full of expectation and male bass and baritone, clipped, but reassuring under the hubbub.

By the time I got home with Grandma, the soup was ready. All she had to do was to throw the pasta she rolled and cut the night before into the boiling broth. On important holidays, Anyu's masterpiece of a walnut cake that used up nine eggs and was covered with a buttery walnut spread decorated with cherries preserved in rum, was also ready and waiting for us on the kitchen table.

I remember the day the rickety dining table in the room was set for a Sunday feast. White linen tablecloth and matching napkins, glasses rubbed until they were so spotless that they reflected the spoons and forks like shiny jewels, the soda syphon with its curved elephant trunk and a small bouquet of short-stemmed carnations in a vase were all in place before Grandma and I left for mass.

Apu and Anyu also arrived back from the tennis court in time for the meal. They always looked happy after tennis. Grandma and I watched the noodles boil while we waited for them to change.

The chicken soup came first with globs of shiny fat floating above the dumplings and the wings, the neck and the pair of feet, which still had the mottled yellow skin attached. The chicken skull, my favourite bit, was a treat reserved for me. I always handed it to Anyu, who smartly split it open with her knife in the middle of the forehead and put the two globs of brain back on my plate.

"It will make you smart," she told me often. And I believed it, because above all else I wanted to be smart.

We had about three spoonfuls of soup when suddenly Apu's fist landed on the table and the glasses started to dance.

"It's cold," he said. "The soup is cold again." He stood up and threw his napkin on his chair. "Can't get a decent hot soup in this house." His voice kept rising, "It's simple enough. The soup must be hot. After all these years it should be clear that I loathe cold soup."

Mother got up and rushed to the bathroom closing the door behind her. I followed her and kept knocking on the door. "Let me in, Anyu!" I found her sitting on the edge of the bathtub. Crying.

I sat down beside her and hugged her.

We could hear the front door slam. After a while we got up and went back to the table to finish our soup. By then it turned colder than lukewarm on our plates.

73

Daisy chains

The lawns of Margit Island were endless green carpets rolled out in front of me, inviting me to run all over them. They seemed to stretch unbounded between the sky and the Danube.

During our summer walks, I could not wait to turn my back to the bench where Anyu chose to sit down with a sigh, clutching her handbag on her lap, ready to rest under the giant trees shading the footpath.

I would glance back only once to make sure that she was there and I was off across the grass, feeling free and at the same time safe under her protection.

Miniature white daisies grew in bright patches. I looked for the densest sweep of flowers, the best spot to squat down and pick the ones with the longest stems. When I had enough gathered in the bowl of my uplifted skirt, I would sit down on the grass, spread my legs and start tying a daisy chain, a skill I learned from Grandma. I braided and knotted a small bracelet for myself and a long necklace for Anyu.

She let me lift it over her head by bending down in front of me and she wore it all the way home, even on the No. 6 streetcar packed with people without flowers.

74

Turntable hypnosis

On stormy Sundays we didn't go anywhere but stayed in the warm cocoon of our tiny flat. The factory yard was deserted, the wind flogged the oleander stalks and the rain drummed on the window. By afternoon, Apu often put down his book and lifted the lid of our black gramophone. I'd stand by him beside the table watching him move the nickel handle and start winding up the invisible spring hidden under the turntable.

Anyu busied herself sorting through the dozen or so records we had and selecting one with Apu's approval. I watched her sliding it out from its paper jacket with care. I had a favourite of my own, rarely played because the two of them more often chose a Khachaturian or Mozart's Eine Kleine Nacht Music than the sweet Irving Berlin song, "The Girl on the Police Gazette".

Apu flicked a small metal bar, and the turntable - a round platter with faded baize cover – slowly started to rotate. This movement in itself was hypnotic as I concentrated on a small ink spot on the edge turning and turning.

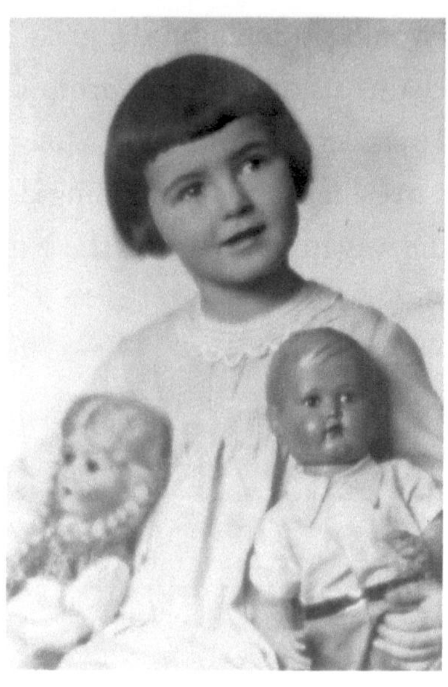

I don't know when we got that record. Was I five or ten? But I know how it cheered me and how it made me skip and move in an inescapable rhythm as I stepped closer to the window in search of wider vistas beyond the line of kitchen windows on the opposite side of the house.

I knew the meaning of English words: girl, police and gazette: *lány, rendőr, ujság*. I was sure that the girl in the song was me and even before I was sent to learn elementary English and had an inkling of the lyrics, I identified with that girl.

"Oh, my search will never cease for the girl on the Police Gazette
For the pretty young brunette on the pink Police Gazette."

Later, in my teens, I promoted her to be a reporter on the gazette, bright and light, sitting by her clattering typewriter, her curls bouncing around her face as she hit the keys with flying fingers composing reports about earthshaking events.

I moved with the music. Mozart was lullaby compared to Irving Berlin.

Kelemen's cap

A tram conductor's blue cap
summons up
the cap of old Kelemen
a similar blue
but moth–eaten
and the hard visor's sheen
already worn away
back in '44

dimmed of shine
like the jug
his wife dipped in the tin bucket
heavy with cool water
lined with green moss

just this
a cap
no more
is enough to bring back

the taste of those days
when I was still
ravenous
free of memories
free of knowing

75

What's in a name?

Through the years my name changed so many times that I should've been confused, but I never was. I came running whatever voice with whatever accent called me by whatever name.

Trying to list all my names requires patience.

To start with, Anyu and Apu addressed me as *Panni*. That was the direct address. "Panni, Panni where are you?" Or: "Just one more spoonful, *Pannika*. Open your mouth. Good girl."

When they talked about me to someone else, they called me *Pankás*. For instance, "Yesterday I took *Pankás* to Margit Island."

If I misbehaved, I became *Pankás Kölyök*.

This translates to "Pankás Rascal", a designation I found delightful enough to make up a rhyme I sang merrily:

"Én vagyok a Pankás Kölyök
Kinek minden csontja zörög."

Roughly translated:

"I am known as Pankás Rascal
jingle-bony and skeletal."

Whether skipping down the stairs or twirling a jump rope in the yard, I sang this with gusto for years, making fun of my skinny frame that was often remarked upon by our acquaintances. "You can count her ribs, she is so thin. How's her appetite?"

In the village of Püski everyone insisted on feeding me, "Eat Pannika! Put on some meat, or you'll blow away in the wind."

From the first day of school, which I started when I was almost seven, my name changed to *Éva*. Officially my Christian names were *Éva Borbála*. That's what my birth certificate said: *Szilágyi Éva Borbála*. None of these had anything to do with Panni. I don't know who or why decided to call me Panni.

It may have been that it was to legitimize Panni (which is one of the endearing pet names for Anna) that Anyu chose Anna as my confirmation name at age nine. A proud Roman Catholic blessed and confirmed by a bishop, I suddenly possessed three Christian names: *Éva Borbála Anna.*

Even today, I am fond of all these names because they slot me into different realities requiring me to respond with different accents, re-enter divergent lives. I consider this propensity neither a weakness nor a vague category of deception. Some may label it adaptive behavior, role-playing, or may call it downright trickery. Such labels are of no interest to me. I know that it has nothing to do with consciously choosing a different persona, and that it originates in my childhood, when I learned to fit in, to give up parts of my life, to play safe by being a chameleon.

76

Alphabet hopping

My last name could also cause confusion.

In first grade I was enrolled as *Szilágyi Éva.*

At the Aréna Road Elementary School our teachers enacted a ritual roll call every morning. Auntie Klemi, our home room teacher, who looked very old with a long neck and salt-and-pepper hair sausages stuck on her head, read out our names and we had to yell: "Present!"

My name was towards the end of the alphabet, and she always started with the letter "a". For some reason I ardently wished to be at the beginning of the alphabet, to have a lovely name like Alcsúti or Apafy, but I was stuck beyond the "p" and "r" names like Pócsa, and Ruzicska. It seemed to be my unalterable fate.

I already knew the alphabet by heart, so after a while I accepted my placement with resignation as justified and proper. I knew that *Szilágyi* meant that you came from the place called *Szilágy*. But, of course, I was born in Budapest, and nobody I knew came from *Szilágy Megye*, a county that today belongs to Romania and is called *Judetul Salaj*.

Then suddenly Szilágyi changed to Palásti.

Jumping two letters in the alphabet pleased me, and I accepted the reason for the change. My father explained that at the paper, where his byline often appeared, there was another *Szilágyi László*, and the editor asked him to change his name not to clash with the older writer. For a while he only used *Palásti* as his pen name, but because all his official documents were under the name of *Szilágyi*, and he had become quite well known as *Palásti*, he decided to avoid the confusion and make the change final and official. At last I jumped in the class roll call ahead of Pócsa.

"Pa" beats "Pó".

Some people managed to interpret the change in an unflattering way. "She changed her father," I overheard whispers behind my back in school. After a while I got tired of giving an explanation.

When I landed in America as a refugee in January 1957 and met my relatives there, to my surprise, they all called me Barbara. It turned out that Ómama, who had corresponded with her sister Berta and her brothers before the war, had announced my birth under that name. She never mentioned Panni or Éva, so I soon learned to respond to my relatives in Maine and California as Barbara.

Since in Latin Barbara means "foreign woman" and is associated with the meaning "barbarian", this could be the name that fits me most.

77

Ambidexterity

I am left-handed. This is supposed to be a handicap. I am made to feel ashamed. In school, my clumsiness may cause a teacher to raise a disciplinary ruler and whack my left hand, making me swiftly switch the pencil into my right.

Apu says that all geniuses are left-handed. He doesn't mean to put Grandma down, but gets annoyed with her when she is nagging me in the kitchen, "Use your other hand!" She grabs the spoon or the knife out of my left. "Let me do it. I can't bear seeing your keck-handed mess."

Apu doesn't know that I don't mind. On the contrary, I am relieved. I can leave the kitchen and the chores behind.

How could I have known that thanks to my ruler-wielding teachers I was on my way to end up with the upper hand of being ambidextrous for the rest of my life?

78

The best place for homework

I am sitting at the dining table with my ruler in one hand and a pencil in the other. The pencil needs sharpening. I get up from Apu's chair, the one with arms and leather upholstery nailed down with brass tacks, the chair of domestic power I like to occupy whenever he is away.

My shiny new pencil sharpener is in the pencil case by my notebook. I pick it up and start to turn it over, carefully holding it above my knees to make sure that the shavings fall into my apron and not on the floor. It doesn't work. The blade chews into the graphite and breaks off the tip. I carry on until the pencil shrinks into a short stub.

I get up holding my apron littered with wood shavings and crumbs of graphite and try to shake them into the rubbish bin in the kitchen.

Grandma looks up from her sewing.

"What's up?"

"The sharpener doesn't work," I open my apron, and she glances at the mess.

"Now you can't wear it tomorrow," she says. "You can't go to school in a dirty apron."

"It's just the pencil..."

"Look at the black spots," she puts down her scissors. "Give me that pencil."

She picks up a knife and with swift strokes sharpens the stub without snapping the graphite. "There," she says. "How much more have you got to do?"

"Not much. Finished the arithmetic yesterday and only have to draw the line design at the end of my new story." I always explain my homework to her in great detail because she likes to hear about school.

Back in father's important chair I consider the pattern I want to draw. Blue waves with a yellow dot under each crescent, red tulips with green leaves floating on top. A new pattern at the end of each home assignment makes my teacher smile. She likes to see pretty ones and often compliments me when she hands back my homework.

School is a place where I can shine. It is a place of clean wide corridors and echoing staircases filled with the buzz of girls' voices. There is order and discipline. I have figured out how to avoid the unpleasant parts, how to show keenness when it is useful.

Our apartment with the afternoon sun filling the room is made for homework. The veneer on the wardrobe reflects the light, the books on the shelf above the bed show off their multi-coloured spines. Apu's marble inkwell with its brass lion sits comfortably on his desk, and a potted geranium in the window is brimming with bright red petals.

Plop-Pop

In praise of distance

You have to go far away
from where you were born
in order to see
the contours of hills
of valleys and peaks
the true size and bias
of church spires
the narrow alleys
of pinched perspectives
and the topography
of self-referential graffiti
etched on each lurching heart.

Insight gets its start
on an indifferent
different continent.

79

Pretty postcards

It turns into winter, and the war is edging closer.

Strings are strung across the nearby tobacconist's window. Clipped to the strings are postcards. Most have a line or two printed under a picture. These black-and-white photographs are colour-enhanced with red smeared on the lips, pink on the cheeks, crimson on carnations in buttonholes.

The captions are short:

"Heart to heart"

"Missing you, sweetheart"

"Waiting for you"

"Thinking of you, darling"

"A message from Motherland"

"No, No, Never!"

"Trianon, Never Again!"

"Onward to Victory"

"Our Chosen Star Is Shining"

"Until I Hold You in My Arms"

"See You Again, Second Lieutenant, Sir"

"Every December Heralds a New May"

I stand on the chill street kicking my heels on the icy sidewalk. A few *filler* coins are gripped hard in my fist. My other hand is buried in my coat pocket. I wear my dark blue coat with shiny gold buttons. Each button has an anchor minted on it. I know it is not real gold, but I feel good, proud of my buttons. My winter coat is warm, although the sleeves are getting shorter and it is getting tight around my chest.

I often linger over the images above the declarations of love and patriotic fervour. Handsome soldiers in impeccable uniforms stare back at me.

One of the postcards shows a troop train. A big black locomotive exhales a cloud of steam, ready to go. The platform is crowded with young men saying goodbye to women, to their sweethearts and mothers. No fathers are visible. In another, an officer stands in front of a burnt-out enemy tank that smolders in a snowy landscape in the infinite winter steppe of the Russian hinterland.

And there is a soldier standing guard at night under an old-fashioned lamppost by an iron gate leading to dark barracks. He is half- obscured by shadows as he looks down on the illuminated upturned face of his girl. Her lips are slightly parted, ready to kiss him good-bye. She is beautiful, a slender goddess standing on tiptoes to reach his mouth. She teeters on her high heels above the wet cobblestones.

That is the one I like best.

I draw her in my exercise books a hundred times. Her profile and her feet, her perfect, slender calves.

I find excuses to go by the tobacconist's shop and stare at the people in these postcards. They talk to me. They tell me stories that make the news of battlefields taste sour-sweet. The lieutenants by the rails, the soldiers on guard in the moonlight seem lost. Looking at them, so handsome, so yearning, I am compelled to make up stories and run them in my head. I can feel their breath on my face. I am that girl on tiptoes under the lamppost.

I am Lili Marlene.

80

Magyar Tőzsde

The national library is the storehouse of everything ever printed in Hungary.

Now I am in the 21st century on a visit to Budapest researching my father's publications.

Culling through disintegrating copies of the newspaper where Apu worked, I find blatant examples of "politically correct" journalism during the war. The following are some short examples from 1940, 1942 and 1944.

In 1940:
Magyar Tőzsde (Hungarian Stock Exchange) 20 January 1940

> "Life insurance companies are hoping that the finance ministry will allow them to retain the services of the few remaining Jewish salesmen until they can train appropriate Christian personnel. This is in accordance with the decrees governing the implementation of the anti-Jewish law."

In 1942:
Magyar Tőzsde, 19 December 1942:

> "HUNGARIAN FINANCIAL INSTITUTIONS ARE IN THE SERVICE OF WARFARE"

> "We are in the fourth year of total war, a war that is justifiably called total because more than 90 per cent of the world's population

participates in it. In this giant struggle Hungary yet again stands as a bulwark of western culture and civilization against the destructive power of the east that is bolshevism..."

In 1944:
The last issue of *Hungarian Stock Exchange in December*:

> The Life Insurance Business Is Booming
>
> "According to the report of the board of directors of the Hermes Hungarian General Exchange Business their balance sheet for 1943-44 shows a 329.500.21-pengő profit compared to a 328.328.77-pengő profit in the previous year."

By then the Soviet army was heading for Berlin and closing its ring around Budapest.

81

Apu's cheap labour

Now, that I am much older than my father was when he died at age 76, I can see reasons for my father's quick temper, his anger.

Coming home for him must have meant entering a tiny apartment above a factory yard, facing a silently disapproving mother-in-law and a wife who had a job and was the continuous steady breadwinner, while he was out of work, a man facing daily humiliations.

It must have been an effort to put on a smiling face and to joke with his noisy daughter whom he could not support. Home had become a place where he daily faced his failure to fulfill the traditional role of the main provider, time-honored head of a family.

Home became a constant reminder of his buried dreams.

He was desperate for any work. He found one place that risked employing him illegally after the anti-Jewish laws made legal work inmpossible. It was a small newspaper called *"Hungarian Stock Exchange"*.

He worked there every chance he got before and after he was drafted into what was hurriedly designated as the "208/21Labour Company", a forced labour unit for Jews.

That newspaper was no Wall Street Journal. Run on a shoestring, it could engage Apu every now and then. The owner was no anti-Semite, and Apu was cheap.

He used to put on his best suit, his freshly ironed poplin shirt with a silk tie and stuff his Montblanc, a Vicki Baum novel and notebooks into his brown leather briefcase, hug me, kiss Anyu and leave in a hurry.

He'd take a train to far provincial towns and interview bankers and factory owners, managers of mines and big landholdings. He came back with news for the paper and a few *pengős* for Anyu to help her pay the rent, the gas, and all the bills I was only vaguely aware of.

He brought back gifts for us. Another Karl May book for me. Or a rubber ball bigger than the last one. For Anyu, maybe a pair of silk stockings or a bottle of perfume. She would protest. What extravagance! But he would hug her, lift her up a bit and say, "My queen deserves the best!"

Anyu would laugh and return his kiss.

All the headlines shouted about the war they called the Second. Anyu told me that she was 12 when the first one started. Apu was the same. They didn't talk to me about those times.

I didn't ask questions. His cheerfulness worked on me as well. Even when I could comprehend the meaning of racism and its effects on my father, I still considered myself exempt. After all, being half-and-half had to be all right.

82

Bathtub thoughts

Lying submerged in soapy water in our bathtub between air raids, I raise my head and study my naked body.

Which part belongs to whom?

Are my legs and thighs Catholic and my arms Jewish? My heart from my mother, my lungs from my father? My head from Grandma? My hips from Ómama?

How could the SS take me apart?

I conclude that it is impossible, that I am safe, that my Aryan parts make me untouchable.

I hang on to my sense of immunity.

Gross Aktion Berdichev

For Vasily Grossman, "A Writer at War"

It was summer when they came.
The trees were green,
plums overripe
birds blackened the sky
stirred up by the line of tanks
that made the earth tremble
and echo over the ravines.

Thunder and clatter bore their approach.
Children ran in, doors slammed, bolted,
whispers damped down behind shutters.

Still there were some who stood outside
offered loaves of bread and salt
to the armoured conquerors.

They were the ones
who helped the round-ups
of tailors, shoemakers,
tinsmiths, doctors,
carpenters, tanners,
water carriers, butchers,
seamstresses, teachers,
mothers with babes in arms,
old men with bent backs,
cripples, expectant brides,
herded with curses and guns.

Schnell, schnell! Bistro!
A brisk wind blew
over the cornfields
where they were ordered to strip
turn and face naked
the freshly dug ditch.
A hungry baby sucked greedily
on his mother's breast.

What's left to us
is to exhume
their stories
left unsaid
by the wordless dead.

83

Don't go, Apu!

When Apu got his call-up paper, it caused chaos in our household. Anyu helped him finish the preparations for his departure.

Our beautifully veneered wardrobe with its curved doors was wide open with our things jumbled up inside. Apu's clothes were scattered on the bed, on the table, on every chair.

He was going.

I asked him where?

"Who knows?" he said.

"We don't want to pack this." Anyu held up a brown scarf. "You will wear it. Put it on now."

"I like the white one better," he said.

"Not practical. Will get dirty right away," Anyu snatched it out of his hand. She was impatient.

He started stuffing shirts into a rucksack. Anyu took them out and folded them properly. "How many?" she asked.

"Six?"

"There is no room for six. You have to take more underwear. Jacket. Raincoat. A hat. Gloves. Warm gloves. Warm socks. Soap. Shaving things…"

"Paper. Pen. Books," Apu added.

"No room for books. Too heavy. Maybe one book. You have to take something to eat. That's more important."

"They must feed us."

"Maybe. But how often? A loaf of bread. Jam. I've packed half a kilo of bacon. A pocket knife. Scissors. A bag of sugar. "

Apu sighed and sat down starting to put on a pair of brand new hobnail boots.

"Damn heavy."

"Get used to it."

He put on the rucksack that made him lean forward. Anyu straightened the armband on his coat. It was a white armband, not yellow like those that Jews had to wear. That much I knew. He had to wear white, meaning that he had converted to the Catholic faith, studied the Catechism for weeks with Anyu and with a priest.

Grandma washed and ironed his armband, but Anyu sewed it.

"Let's go," he said.

Going down the stairwell, his boots made a lot of noise. It was obvious that he was not happy going on this trip.

"Where are the mountains you will climb?" I asked again standing at the gate, looking at his boots.

He reached out to hug me. "Who knows?"

"Why can't I go with you?"

"They only want men. You stay home. Be a good girl."

He turned and held Anyu longer than he held me.

Fifty years later, when I knew much more about the mountains he had climbed, I wrote this poem:

In praise of boots

On feet caked with the mud of miles,
river grit, dung and clinging burr,
bent under tattered rucksacks,
string-tied bundles sodden with endless rain
men march in strict lines.
Blood blisters, lice, the reek of unwashed shirts
and dirty foot clouts around
swollen ankles and frostbitten toes
dog them as the road twists
around mountain peaks.

Then they hear "Halt!"
The guards rest and feed the horses
that haul a creaking carriage
laden with rations under a tarpaulin.
Horses are useful, they must be treated right.

The boots blunder on with gaping soles,
flap open and slap at each step.
More precious than diamonds or gold,
they are the last hold, a thin shield from pain,
gangrene and a grave in a ditch by the road.

84

The sound of sirens

When air raid sirens were introduced in Budapest, and we first heard the rising and falling sound of the new alarm, my first thought was that we were keeping up with the modern world, getting what London and Berlin already had. Our clever authorities were looking after us with the latest gadgets. People got busy sweeping clean their cobwebbed cellars, whitewashing the walls, carrying down pillows and chairs to sit there in safety and comfort.

The first air raid drills in school were welcome interruptions. Class after class filed down to the basement and sat down on the new wooden benches lined up against the walls. We sat quietly while a teacher spoke about the heroic sacrifices of our men fighting against the barbaric hordes of the East. She urged us to bring from home any leftover skeins of wool we could find, so that we could knit warm socks and send them to our men in Russia where the winter was incredibly cold.

Sometimes we sang a song as we filed back to our class, and we felt good together stepping in unison, unafraid and protected by our heroes. My medal pinned to my apron seemed to me almost identical to a military medal won by a soldier, even if mine was only for being the best speller last week.

85

A song we sang in school

There was a song, a joyous melody. We sang it tapping our feet because it had an irresistible marching rhythm expressing the confidence of triumphant armies.

"Szabadka, Zombor, Ujvidék.
Honvédsereg ma virágra lép...
Visszatért szép Délvidékünk..."

Délvidékünk means the southern area that was carved off Hungary as punishment by the calamitous Trianon Treaty, the end result of being on the losing side in the First World War.

And the next line went:

"*Visszaadta Horthy nékünk.*"

"*Horthy nékünk*" rhymes beautifully with "*Délvidékünk*".

In English (roughly paraphrased) this song recites the names of three cities Hungary re-occupied in Yugoslavia when our government, the same government that had signed a non-aggression treaty pledging 'eternal friendship' with that same country just four months before, decided to cross its borders. Of course, I had no idea about the ins-and-outs of geopolitics, and didn't know that Hitler promised us those towns as a reward for helping him.

The second line of the song states that our soldiers walk on flowers as they cross the border and enter the newly liberated beautiful southern territory.

Soldiers in general seem to have a strong desire to walk on carpets of flowers all through the ages, all through the world.

Did the Greeks walk on flowers on the streets of Troy?

Did flowers blanket the mud of Passchendaele in 1917?

The streets of Stalingrad?

Or the icy banks of the Danube in December 1945?

Rivers ran red with the blood of the slaughtered throughout Hungarian history. How many times? How many battles had been won? How many wars lost?

There are things we try to forget, to wipe from our collective memory. The more we try, the more they haunt us.

Yes, I sang that song with enthusiasm. And others like it.

Songs can dazzle and blind.

I am surrounded by the sounds of:

the Radetzky March on the radio
stories of battles told and retold
church bells ringing for dead souls
the tunes of "The Merry Widow"
Lili Marlene
the songs of Snow White and the Seven Dwarfs
speeches at presentations of medals on newsreels
stories of strategic withdrawals on icy roads
flapping flags snapping on parades
the marching thump of conscripted men
military salutes with boots clicking
harangues from flag-draped balconies
Governor Horthy's white horse sneezing
Heil! Heil! and Heil again!
stormy applause as Hitler mounts various podiums
the silence of uniformed amputees
Viennese waltzes streaming through open windows
snap-snap of posters with new proclamations
the murmur of anxious people reading the posters

the soft swish of egret feathers on old-fashioned hats
oompah-oompah bands playing in squares
the pleas of beggars on church steps and street corners
the hum of Mercedes classics carrying German officers
the whispers of not-so-merry war widows
praying in church pews

86

An ambulance arrives

My elbows rest on the windowsill.

It is late afternoon, and I am waiting for Anyu.

The machines are humming behind the dusty factory windows to my right. The big gate opens to the left, to let Gebhardt pedal through on his tricycle. The courtyard is empty, so it is easy for him to manoeuvre to the lean-to where the tricycle spends the night. The paint is peeling on the sides of its plywood hold, but I don't need to read it, having learnt it by heart way back when I was four years old and started to read: *Baum Adolf és Társa, Kft.* Should I translate it for you? Adolf Baum and Partner Ltd, the name of the factory.

It is time for Anyu to come for me.

I am dressed in my best Scottish plaid skirt with a pure white blouse, black patent leather shoes and spotless white socks. I also have a small, military-style cap (or is it authentic Scottish?) matching my skirt. It is sitting on the top of the sewing machine, ready for me.

I don't much like that cap: cocky, narrow, designed not to stay on my head, needing to be secured with a tight elastic band that regularly raises a red welt under my chin.

I am told that it has to be worn with my Scottish skirt. It is the right thing to do and I like to do the right thing, especially the visibly right thing. My omissions and transgressions I keep hidden.

"We'll be late," I say.

Grandma doesn't answer. She is standing outside, on the balcony, swinging an iron, a smoking pendulum, trying to get the fire going. I see the sparks flying. She bends down, opens the lid and adds some more charcoal before she resumes drawing half-circles in the air, her right arm going back and forth, back and forth.

The sun has gone down. Grandma finishes ironing. She is folding the sheets and pillowcases.

"Where is she?" I grumble. "It's late." I rub my stiff knees, not sure whether to be pleased about being late for the dentist whom I dread, or to be annoyed by Anyu. My tartan skirt's halters are tight over my shoulders and my patent leather shoes, now outgrown, pinch my big toes.

"Yes," Grandma answers at last. She empties the ashes from the iron into the garbage. "I guess you are going to miss your appointment." She looks worried.

Anyu told me in the morning that she'd be here at four o'clock.

These were her exact words: "I've told Fülöp that I'll take off at three thirty. I can make up that hour and a half on Saturday."

Good at maths, I can calculate the distribution of the 48 hours Anyu has to work in the offices of Zsigmond Büchler and Partner in the Budapest Stock Exchange.

"He'll be furious," I say meaning the dentist, a friend of Apu. Everybody is a friend of Apu. Everybody owes him a favour, or is owed a favour, I am not sure which, as the two directions seem perpetually interchangeable.

I take off my shoes and wiggle my liberated toes.

"There must be a good reason," Grandma puts away the ironing board and proceeds tightening the poppy seed grinder on the edge of the kitchen table. "She'll come, sooner or later," she says. "I remember back in 1915 when she was late from school one day and I…"

She stops to listen to the noise coming from the direction of the gate.

Voices, doors banging, an engine coming to a halt.

I run out to lean over the balcony rail. Grandma follows wiping her hands on her apron. I feel a shiver going down my spine and see a pair of sharp headlights illuminating the steps below me.

They are the lights of an ambulance. Mr Kelemen is bending low by its open door. Three men are lifting out a stretcher. And when the stretcher is carried around the headlights, I can see a pale face above a grey blanket, a face that looks vaguely like Anyu's. Grandma puts a hand on my shoulder, but I shake it off and run to the stairs. Taking them two by two, I reach the ground floor in time to see four men, each holding one arm of the stretcher, lift Anyu above their head and start to climb the stairs slowly, carefully.

One hand, the one with her gold wedding band - the ring you can see me wear today on my right hand - dangles scraping against the wall of the stairwell as the men slowly carry her upstairs.

I am following them, wanting to hold that pale hand, but I can't, there is no room around the bends of the steps.

They put Anyu down in the middle of the room, while Grandma busies herself spreading sheets, throwing pillows - what seems like a blizzard of white linen - over the double bed. She mumbles, an insistent murmur that punctuates each movement, "God, my God! Virgin Mary! Our Father! My God!"

Other voices start to penetrate.

A male choir, the ambulance men's voices.

"Streetcar. She just walked into it. Hit her back."

"Lucky, she fell outward, not on the rails."

"Not under the wheels. Bruises, not many cuts. A little bleeding."

"Maybe the spine, the doctor said."

"Concussion."

"The conductor says she wasn't looking. He wasn't going too fast. He kept banging on the bell."

They lift Anyu and place her on the bed. That's when she makes the first sound. An agonizing moan.

I am standing by the window, now totally dark, trembling. I never thought of that.

Her spine. A streetcar made of steel on steel rails. Rolling on steel wheels. The squeal of steel on steel. The screech of brakes. The clanging of the bell.

I am sure that I've thought of everything. I've tried so hard while I was waiting. Thought of Fülöp in his tight tweed jacket with the leather elbow patches, his balding head and red moustache, fat Fülöp keeping her in late because of an urgent letter needing to go out. I thought of sirens, an air raid that forced her to go into a cellar on the way home. No. Air raids take in the whole city. She would have been in a cellar as well as us and the dentist and everyone else in Budapest. Air raids cancel lateness, excuse everything.

I thought that she might have fainted. That happened sometimes. The cause was exhaustion. That's what Anyu said to Grandma one day.

I even thought of an accident. But not a streetcar. I forced myself to envision a car accident in painstaking detail, one of those big automobiles going too fast on the *Körút*, one of those big black cars with the spare wheel sitting by the front wheel, a convertible filled with German officeers who act like they own the place.

I forgot to think about streetcars. It is always what you forget to worry about that happens. Standing behind the stretcher, hidden behind the backs of the ambulance men who are gathering up straps and blankets, ready to depart, ready to pick up the next victim of another misfortune, I suddenly feel that I can't move closer, can't look at the face of my mother.

Why did I forget to ward off streetcars?

Why did I fail her?

plop-pop

on our roof
rain drops play
pop-plops

drum along
blessed rain
come again
feed our streams
raise our grain

plop-pop
plop-pop
each raindrop
tastes so good
on my tongue

then one day
dry pop-pops
come our way

first a few far away
then many
every day

can't go out
have to crawl
underground
get away
from loud pops
all around

now I don't
want to hear
any more
any kind
of pop-pop
stop it
stop
stop

87

They carry Anyu

When the sirens sound, Grandma wraps Anyu in a blanket.

She makes one corner cover her head and the opposite corner tucked in around her feet. The other two corners tightly swaddle her the way they swaddle babies.

She is careful when she rolls her from side to side, trying not to bend her spine where the streetcar bumped her.

Anyu bites her lower lip, but there is not a peep out of her.

Then we wait until Mr Bauer and Mr Kelemen arrive with a stretcher. They place her on top and carry her down the stairs. Grandma and I follow with our bundles.

The five of us are always the last to get inside before Mr Bauer closes the shelter door.

For weeks they carry her, until she is well enough to slowly walk down the stairs herself.

Grandma and I pray for her recovery.

Mary, mother of Jesus, please, listen to me.

Soon, she limps back to work at the Stock Exchange again.

88

The power of documents

In the summer of 1944, I finished my fourth year in elementary school with a report card of straight 'A's. I had a clean slate to enter a gymnasium, a prep school for university. I was proud of my results.

When I handed my report card to Anyu, I expected praise and a big hug.

I was taken aback when my mother shook her head looking at the first page of the report. There, under my name, a school administrator had crossed out Rk, *Roman Catholic* in the rubric of religion and replaced it with *Izr*, an abbreviation meaning *Izraelita.*

Anyu said that this was a malicious mistake and meant trouble.

Undaunted, she made an appointment to meet the head of *Ráskay Lea Gimnázium*. She took time off from work and went there to ask for my enrolment. When she came home she was upset and stayed quiet until I pressed her to explain what happened.

"We must hide your report card," she said. "It can get us in trouble."

"Why? Was he mean to you?

"No, he is a decent man. He said that he would be happy to have you as a student, but because of your religion he was prohibited to enroll you. There was no way. He couldn't break a new law and enroll a Jew."

Soon after this encounter, Anyu packed us up and took Grandma and me to the village of her birth. Everybody knew there that I was a confirmed Roman Catholic, and we were safe, not only from the bombs.

While we were packing, deciding what to take and what to leave, we were witnessing another kind of packing, the preparations of our Jewish neighbours to move out of the house.

89

From the mouth of a child

The noises of the bomb shelter, the coughing, the cursing, the sighing, the snoring and the whispered prayers during the brief lulls between detonations were reassuring. They were human noises.

We were jammed together regardless of religions. We trudged down the steps together with the Jewish Kendes, the Baums, old and young, including diabetic Mrs Baum leaning on the arms of her son and husband.

There was no talk, we listened to the noises in the sky.

Grandma was silently praying. I could tell by looking at her lips trembling under her closed eyes.

Mr Kelemen snored in the old armchair he had carried down into the cellar for his wife. Too wide to fit into it, she preferred to lie on a mattress and ordered him to sit instead.

I felt comforted listening to the officious commands of our shelter commander, Mr Bauer, who never took off his armband and seemed to be attached to his rubber truncheon, a tool of his authority. I was sure that he knew how to keep us alive. His wife hummed to their small daughter in her arms.

The child was restless. Then suddenly she spoke up, her voice clear and loud, "It stinks in here! Awful Jewish stink."

I sat across from Mrs Kende. She remained silent, motionless, looking at her hands. Nobody said a word.

Mrs Bauer kept on humming into the ear of her daughter, rocking her as if nothing had happened.

I am glad I am not a Jew, I thought, snuggling closer to Grandma.

Apu was a Jew, but he is not any longer. He's turned Roman Catholic. Besides, he is away with his battalion, he is not here. And he doesn't stink. He bathes almost every day. And he even uses a cologne from Cologne. He always smells good.

Then I thought, the Baums don't smell either. Nor the Kendes. They all have bathrooms.

Soon after that, all the Jews were away, and there was room to put more mattresses down.

90

Kitty's white linen dress

So much happened in the few weeks before we left Budapest.

New laws passed in quick succession turned our neighbourhood upside down. When the Baums were about to move to a house freshly designated for Jews, young Mrs Baum knocked on our door. Anyu was at work, so she talked to Grandma. This was the first time she entered our apartment. Come to think of it, neither Grandma, nor my parents ever entered theirs. For me it was different. I could come and go there when I played with Kitty. Children were free to cross class thresholds.

I didn't hear what she said, because she talked into Grandma's ear, as if she was telling a secret.

When Anyu got home, Grandma said, "Mrs Baum came by this morning."

"What did she want?"

Grandma put her index finger against her lips and pulled aside the kitchen curtain to check the corridor before she spoke quietly. "She will bring a suitcase tonight for safekeeping."

I was already in bed when the suitcase was delivered, not by Mrs Baum but by the assistant concierge who lived in the loft at the top of the staircase. She had free lodging because she worked for the Baums, who owned the house.

Anyu hid the suitcase under the bed and covered it with a blanket. Some weeks later when she managed to hire a truck for our move to the village, the suitcase was loaded on it alongside our best pieces of furniture and our own suitcases, all tightly rammed together into an unsteady heap and tied down with ropes.

The driver was a bald man who hardly said a word, just nodded his head at whatever Anyu asked him to do, but he was strong, he could lift and carry anything on his back down the staircase. His truck blocked the entrance, but nobody complained. The air raids made

everyone reconciled to disorder. Mr Kelemen himself gave a hand and protested when Grandma tried to lift too much.

Our trip westward was not easy. During one air raid the driver tried to park the truck under a tree, out of sight, and the tyres got stuck in the mud. We had to gather twigs to stuff under the treads to get a grip, and stop it spinning in place.

Another time a back wheel started to rattle. Rat-tat-tat-tat. Grandma and I were sitting on the top of a mattress on the back of the truck. Only Anyu had a seat next to the driver. They couldn't hear us shouting, so I had to crawl over a stack of chairs to bang on the top of the cab and alert the driver to stop. He found that the right back wheel was ready to fall off. It took more than an hour to fix it. While the driver puffed and cursed, Anyu told us to sit in the ditch because we were close to a big factory processing bauxite.

"A prime bombing target," she said.

The ditch was full of wildflowers, but I didn't pick any.

Soon we joined the string of evacuee vehicles. Some people, like us, were fleeing from the bombs falling in the cities to the safer countryside, while others, who still thought that Hitler's "wonder weapons" would win the war in the end, were carrying on to Germany.

We arrived in Püski on a hot day. Uncle Pista had a hard time piling all our belongings into their only room in the farmhouse. Some lighter stuff had to be carried up the ladder into the loft. The chairs ended up in the hay above the cowshed.

I totally forgot about the Baum's suitcase until weeks later when Anyu sniffed a smell of mould in the bed she shared with Grandma. She sprung into action with the help of Auntie Terus, stripping all the beds and taking the mattresses outside. They hung them over the hedgerow to air in the sun.

When they opened the two windows facing the street to air the room, Anyu hauled out everything stored under beds including the Baums' suitcase. She noticed that it was also damp and opened it to air out its contents. Everything in it was carefully wrapped in tissue papers. It turned out that they were clothes, most of them belonging to Kitty. As Anyu unwrapped a lace-trimmed white blouse, I remembered Kitty wearing it, her face flushed, sitting at the head of their big table surrounded by friends at her birthday party.

It needed to be hung out in the sun as well.

I helped to unfold rolled up stockings, brown, black, white, hardly worn. I shook out the wrinkles of fine cotton underwear, everything a bigger size than what I could wear. There was a black velvet dress with wonderfully rich and shiny nap that felt smooth to the touch. I could not resist rubbing it against my cheek. And there was a white linen dress with navy stripes on its collar. I had seen her in it on a hot summer day as she was running down the stairs to go somewhere. I held it up against my breast and walked towards the mirror above the chest of drawers brought from Budapest. It was wrinkled, but just the right length and it was loose without a waistline.

I turned to Anyu.

"Just once, could I put it on?"

She smiled.

"Please, Anyu! I'll be careful. Just once."

"I guess, there's no harm," she said as she lifted a nightgown that must have been Mrs Baum's.

I put on the dress, buttoned it up and started to pirouette in front of the mirror.

"It needs ironing," Grandma said.

"Can I wear it to church on Sunday? Just once!"

"Ask your mother."

Anyu hesitated and then slowly said, "If you are careful and don't stain it. And if you take it off right after church and fold it nicely to put it away."

Early next morning, Terike was standing by the kitchen table, engaged in her usual hurried Sunday morning ritual of ironing her father's shirt and the frocks for herself and her mother. When she picked up Kitty's dress, Grandma stood over her. She insisted on wetting a big handkerchief and moving it around under the hot iron to make sure that Terike didn't scorch the precious linen.

I loved Sundays in Püski. Everybody dressed in their best. Everybody stepped out about the same time to go to church. The sidewalks, carefully swept clean the night before, filled up with people politely wishing good morning to each other, women with clean kerchiefs and prayer books in hand, men lifting their dark hats in greeting and small children scrubbed and combed, held in their older sisters' arms or led by the hand.

Before the war, young men stood in bunches near the church gawking at girls who walked arm-in-arm pretending not to care. Now only a few were left because they were deemed unfit to fight. I didn't look at them, but stared straight ahead, sure that they took note of my beautiful white dress.

Older men looked careworn as they stood in front of the church with their heads hanging as they exchanged news. Uncle Pista, who could speak with contempt about drunken priests as often as about the unfit government when we were sitting in the kitchen at dinnertime, joined them wearing his best pair of boots and dark navy suit, dignified as always.

The church was filled with the scent of flowers and smoking candles lit by the statues of saints. Grandma also lit one and put it at the foot of Saint Antal. I dipped my fingers in the stone bowl filled with blessed water and crossed myself doing a proper curtsy.

The harmonium signalled the beginning of mass and I joined a line of girls making sure that I stood close to Terike. She made me feel secure among so many bigger locals.

I quickly turned the pages of the hymnal and held it up so that she could also read the verses, which she didn't need because she knew them all by heart. I tried to sing along knowing that I was often out of tune, as I had been told umpteen times by the music teacher back in Budapest. Still, whenever we came to a long-held note, I was sure that eventually I'd arrive at the right sound and could let my voice boldly rise towards heaven. I felt the joy of being part of a big congregation.

Wearing Kitty's fine dress with its big mother-of-pearl buttons shining on my breast raised that Sunday into a new dimension. God will surely listen. He must see how beautiful I am.

On the way home, Anyu took a picture with Apu's camera of me and Terike standing in front of the school.

Later that year, when the weather turned cold, Grandma let me wear two pairs of Kitty's stockings. "By the time we get back, they'll be too small for her anyway," she said.

Anyu said nothing, but she never let me wear the white dress again.

91

The cow and I

In Püski I learned more about modesty than I learned in Budapest. Even in 1944, when seven of us were thrown together in Uncle Pista's one-room mud house, I never encountered anyone naked. Back in Budapest, if I unexpectedly opened the bathroom door upon Apu, he quickly wrapped a towel around himself, and if I saw Anyu in the bathtub, she would only have soap bubbles on the top of the water to cover her private parts. As a child, my nakedness was natural, totally overlooked.

Not so in Püski, where the men were allowed to strip to the waist but no further to wash after work in the kitchen, but women were obliged to perform their ablutions in the cowshed. Here from an early age I was considered to be a woman.

Terike, who was older than I, filled a *lavór* with warm water for me in the kitchen and carried it across the yard to the shed together with a towel and a bar of soap. She placed it on the milking stool beside the quietly masticating cow, ordered me to undress and to soap my body all over with a soapy rag by the time she came back with my fresh change of clothes.

The shed belonged to me alone, unless I counted the cow that was totally self-absorbed and paid no attention to me other than granting an occasional side-glance. I had undisturbed time to study my body, long-limbed and skinny, a body that had been changing every year and which I was told to keep away from prying eyes. Pride, shame and delight were mixed with the scent of soap, and I enjoyed taking my time rubbing myself, fully aware of the importance of heels and armpits, the back of the neck and the slit between my buttocks, areas needing extra diligence.

As I rinsed off the soap, it was interesting to watch a puddle forming under my bare feet and slowly merging with the puddle of piss spreading from under the cow, with whom I felt a growing intimacy. I turned to study the way her hide twitched on her haunch every time a fly landed there and started biting. No matter how hard I tried, I could not move my skin anywhere on my body that way. Only my face shared this ability.

92

Uncle Géza

My summers in Uncle Pista's house gave me a chance to immerse myself in village life. Farmers were different, less talkative, less hurried, more inscrutable than the people I knew in Budapest. It was harder for me to read their faces.

Of the five children in the house, Géza was the most mysterious. He rarely spoke, moved with inborn grace and minimal effort. He worked all day without complaint and without apparent joy.

I hardly talked to him, and he never addressed me directly. He was rarely home in the evenings. I think he already had a girl somewhere or was out with other young men of his age at the pub.

When he died, the first to die of the five, he grew in my mind into the symbol of the millions of soldiers slaughtered in the war.

The photo taken after his enlistment party, a portrait with a hint of a smile in his eyes, focuses attention on his hat weighed down with a big bunch of ribbons. Each of these had been tied on by a girl of the village farewelling her favourite recruit. One of them could have become his wife. This, his last photo, is a memento I keep.

Uncle Géza was born in the unlucky year of 1922 in the village of Püski. He was unlucky because by the 1940s he was old enough to be drafted and sent to the front.

He was the firstborn child of my great-uncle Pista, a farm labourer, and Aunt Tera who raised four more children, two girls and two boys.

Their lives of endless toil in respectable poverty was spent on a small section in the edge of the village among thatched and whitewashed cottages built on a newly-formed lane appropriately named New Row. I was told that their small, flood-prone parcel of land was recently divested and subdivided by the Roman Catholic Church, traditional owner of vast tracts across the country.

Géza attended the village school, a white adobe building that offered six years of education at the time. The children were taught in one room with the teacher taking turns to address each grade level sitting in separate rows.

By the 20th century, illiteracy was no longer common. Géza also benefited from the enlightened views of his father, who was a veteran of the First World War and, as such, "travelled" abroad. Wars were the only chance for the poor to see the world beyond the village horizon.

In the service of the unraveling Habsburg empire, Uncle Pista was captured and dragged all over Russia as a prisoner of war. He had a lot of stories to tell about the vast steppes and great rivers, about the drab cities and scattered villages, about the hopes of a revolution, the hunger and the hardships. He talked about the compassion of peasants who had nothing to spare, but spared just the same, and about his long hard road back to Püski in the postwar chaos.

I was a lucky child to hear about some of his adventures while we sat around the table in his house after dinner. The flickering light of a petroleum lamp cast moving shadows on the thick adobe walls and enhanced the images of muddy roads, of peasant women letting him milk their cows and chop their wood, inviting him in from the cold to sleep in their wood huts along the way, the windswept, snowbound steppes and of the bedraggled, desperate men trying to make their way back home. He learned Russian due to the First War, and this knowledge stood him in good stead at the end of the Second.

I asked Géza's youngest sister, Terike, to tell me about her brother's time in the army. This is what she wrote down for me (in Hungarian) before she died in a retirement home in 2009 when she was 81:

Géza Markó
Born in Püski: 28 08 1922

Having finished six grades of education at age 12, he started work at the Gallasz estate as an unskilled labourer. He was drafted into service as a frontier guard and served first in Rajka and later in Albertkazmérpuszta.

After the occupation of Sub-Carpathia, he was transferred to Léva. It was from there that he arrived at the line of fire in Transylvania, at Nagyszalonta, where he was wounded, but was not given leave to get home. In October 1944 he was wounded again, but was not allowed home even then.

Just before Szálasi came to power, there were a few hours of ceasefire that lasted long enough for the Hungarian soldiers to get acquainted with the Russians they faced, and they had dinner together. Then they were ordered to turn into enemies again and had to shoot at each other. We thought that this turn had affected him badly. An occasional postcard arrived from him, but we couldn't answer because his address changed continually.

On February 15, 1945, they brought him home with 40 degrees of fever due to a grenade shrapnel that was lodged in his thigh above the knee. He had to stay in bed for two weeks. My mother tried to quench his fever with cold compresses and mugs of tea, because the military doctor said that there was nothing he could do. The army had run out of medication.

Soldiers came to our house every day from headquarters to make sure that we were not trying to hide him away. They said that if we did that, they would execute the whole family in front of Géza.

But where could we hide him when he was so sick? There was no hiding place in our kitchen and our room. And we were afraid of the consequences.

The villagers did hide some of the boys in the surrounding forests, but those were all fit and healthy 15 and 18-year-olds who could easily move around in the woods, not like our Géza who had high fever and who could not possibly survive in the bitter winter cold.

Then they came to take my brother back to the front on the 15th of March. They bundled him onto a horse-drawn carriage heading towards Veszprém. We dressed him in lots of underwear we had warmed first by the fire, then put on his uniform. My mother ran back to the house to get one more blanket to cover him. A sick man was thrown back into battle.

By that time the front moved close to Lake Balaton. The surrounding area had changed hands many times between the Germans and the Russians resulting in many victims on both sides including the Hungarian army, as well as among civilians. An exploding mine killed Géza in Balatonaliga on March 23rd.

We were not notified officially until 1947 when we received his papers. In the same year, a young man from Lipót, a neighbouring village, came to tell us that he was with him when he died.

Before that year, we corresponded a lot with the Red Cross and with the head notary of the region, but we only received negative answers. There were so many of the dead buried in mass graves, that the collection of data and identification took a long time and caused a lot of painstaking work. If they found papers on the bodies, they sent them to the relatives.

My mother travelled to Balatonaliga many times searching and hoping in vain to find his grave.

93

Only the old and the lame left

The village has changed.

Before the war, the seasons rotated with peaceful regularity, work depended on the weather, long dark nights changed into long summer days, men and women carried equal burdens. They celebrated harvests with festivals, with handmade paper flowers decorating the halls. There was music and dances, feasts and wine.

Now, women weep in church for their husbands and sons killed on the Russian front. There are no fit young men left on the streets, only the old, the lame and the addled. There are soldiers coming and going in the barracks at the end of the road, but they are grim strangers plucked form other parts of the country, out of place, wishing to be back home.

"They are afraid to die now, that the war is almost over," Aunt Tera says.

94

Terike in moonlight

The wind and the Moon conspired to make shaking cherry tree branches send sharp beams of light wrestling with shadows through the window. They seemed like ghosts prowling around the room, sliding over the sleeping bodies around me.

The village seemed to be drowning in death. There was the young Polish refugee grabbed by a whirlpool with his hand grasping the air for the last time before he sank.

People talked about a dead English pilot shot down during an air raid knocking on doors begging for food. They whispered about mud-splattered soldiers hovering by the gate trying to get in, soldiers who were killed in the Ukraine. And people saw their long-buried ancestors rising from their graves to deliver warnings.

Pale faces and skulls slowly populated my mind.

I didn't dare to go outside to pee in the middle of the night. I nudged Terike beside me until she stopped snoring and turned towards me.

"I have to go to the long drop."

"Well, get going."

"I can't go. I don't dare."

"I'll go with you then."

"You are not afraid?"

"Afraid? Why should I be?"

The shadows were just as busy in the yard. A distant dog howled.

I was shivering and held on tight to Terike's hand.

"Don't be silly. It's just the Bodó's old dog."

Just then I saw her other hand suddenly dab the sign of the cross on her chest.

When I die

When I die
I'll take with me every tune I've heard
every embrace and every word
every child I've held in my arms
and all the kisses given and taken
sacred vows and false alarms
passing passions
that feed an eternal flame
the fierce faith of youth
and what later came
sweet forgiveness of blows
that missed their mark
and taught me about
the shades of dark.

I'll take reluctant winter sunsets
as they dissolve over the hills
the wistful tenderness of men
too shy to ask
candle-lit tables
laden with manna and wine
I'll take the whole show
profane
divine
it has been mine.

95

News from the Russian front

My great-grandma Ekker bore seven healthy children starting in 1882. Grandma was the oldest of them. Her youngest sister was christened Ilonka, whom I knew well. She was three years younger than my mother, her niece.

Anyu's young aunt lived in Moson, in a big house built by war prisoners captured during the First World War. It was a squat one-storey house that to me looked like a stone monument to hardship. Half of it served as the laundry for the surrounding housing estate of similarly grim bigger houses, and the other half was Auntie Ilonka's one-room-plus-kitchen flat. In there she was raising three children with her husband, Uncle Józsi, a muscular electrician who liked to whistle the latest tunes and to make us children laugh.

Brooding women carrying cane baskets loaded with laundry came and passed silently over the flagstones of a wide corridor where the smell of ammonia lingered in the damp air. This smell penetrated Auntie Ilonka's kitchen and competed with the frying fish she often served us at midday.

The few times we stopped there on our way to Püski, I could hardly wait to move on to the village where I was surrounded by fruit trees, animals and open fields instead of flat grass and cement.

When the war started, Uncle Józsi was conscripted and shipped to the Russian front. My aunt was left to raise their three children alone. Just like Grandma, she started washing and ironing for money. When we visited her in 1944, we huddled in her kitchen during air raids.

"I have no proper cellar under this house," she said. "We'd have to run far, across the lawn to a two-storey house for shelter. It's of no use."

She looked tired and gaunt, her goitrous neck stood out more under her chin.

The next day, before we went on to Püski, Anyu asked her, "When did you hear it?"

These were Aunt Ilonka's words, the way I remember them:

> I was in the kitchen when the man knocked on the door.
>
> I opened the door, and he handed me a piece of paper.
>
> The paper read: "We are sorry to inform you that your husband is missing in action."
>
> "Is he dead?" I asked.
>
> "We don't know," said the man. "I wish I had an answer. Some are dead. Some we never find. Never know."
>
> "Never?"
>
> "He may be alive. He may be a prisoner of war."
>
> The man left. I closed the door and cried.

I cried and cried. Now we were left on our own.

What could I say to the children?

Your father is missing in action?

Your father may not come home?

Your father may be dead? Or he may not?

When they came home from school and we sat down to eat, I said:

"Your father is lost."

We all started crying.

Jenő, the youngest, came to me and hugged me. Then he said:

"Why are we crying, Mother?"

I understood that he didn't understand.

Several years passed before another man arrived at her door.

Auntie told us the story of this man repeatedly after the war as we sat around the table in her quiet house. The story of this second man stayed with me for years. I must have added words to it, and it grew into a more and more vivid picture, a more and more emotional tangle. "Missing in action" is a phrase afloat in my head with incessant echoes.

Only a poem can do justice to my aunt:

Missing in action

his crutches leave dents in the snow
either side of dragging boot prints
two boots on two wooden feet
that replaced two lost in retreat
in the ravenous Russian frost

he is years late but his news
is as raw and fresh as today's
I was with him he says
we walked side by side
no food left nor bullets for guns
carved up and ate our horses
in the relentless icy blizzard
Siberia's revenge

I harassed him
you are lagging behind
tanks are right at our heels
must move on
don't slow down
think of home
gave him half the crust
I found in my pocket
he said nothing
sank into the snow
closed his eyes above his frozen nose
his fingers black and swollen
I swear there was nothing else I could do

I shook him
tried to turn up his collar
but it was stiff with ice
saw what could be called a smile
I knew he was about to die
take my boots he whispered
yours are torn
take them
then he said your name Ilona
Ilona
Ilona
then his head fell back
I changed boots and kept going

that smile
and your name
seen it countless times
calling mother
calling the names of women
delirium and that smile
they say the pain stops
they feel warm
in the lap of mothers and lovers
they are at rest
coming home crippled is harder

Ilona feeds him
makes him a warm bed
he stays for a week telling and retelling
stories of guns and mud and blood
soaks the stumps
what's left of his legs
and the last day he hands her a ring
he says he got from her husband
who ripped it off his frozen finger

Ilona thanks him for telling
and bringing the news and the ring
through miles of snow storms
enemy lines
camps
hospitals
on protheses
for finding the house of his dead friend
although she knows at first glance
that the ring is the wrong ring
that it came off another hand

96

A one in a million chance

Feeling excluded, all but unwanted was a new experience for me.

The sudden silences whenever I entered the house in Püski unnerved me. So did the frequency of being sent outside.

"Isn't it time to feed the chickens, Panni?"

Or: "Can you go and get some more water?"

Off I went to the well to fill the bucket. As I turned the wheel that lowered the creaking chain into the water and turned to look, I saw Anyu through the open door talking passionately. As I re-entered, she was quiet again.

Usually I slept like a log, but one night I woke up suddenly and saw Anyu get out of bed and dress in the dark.

"What's wrong?" I whispered towards her mindful not to wake Terike who was snoring beside me.

Anyu bent down to whisper in my ear. "We are going to Moson, to the market. To sell stuff. Don't worry."

I wanted to ask what they were taking to market. What was there to sell? Corn? I heard Uncle Pista say that there was hardly enough for the animals. Sausages? Or the last smoked ham still hanging in the attic?

Before I could say any of this, Anyu kissed my forehead and was out of the door followed by Aunt Tera, who was wrapped in her big black shawl that reached below her waist. I stared at the moonlight slanting through the window for a while, then I turned to the wall and fell back to sleep.

When I woke again and opened the door just a crack, Grandma

was in the kitchen sieving the fresh milk and talking to Uncle Pista, who was sitting at the table dipping his bread into his coffee mug. I stayed hidden behind the door and listened to Grandma talking under her breath.

“I am more worried every day. When will all this end?”

“They are crazy. I told Tera, but she’s like that. Stubborn.” said Uncle.

“So is my daughter. But he’s her husband, after all.”

“There is a one in a million chance. She has no idea,” Uncle scraped his chair on the floor as he stood up.

“Well, they always come back with their baskets empty,” Grandma’s voice was hardly audible over the drumming of the milk in the churn.

“They can’t feed them all,” he said heading out. “We haven’t got enough to feed them all.”

“Feed whom?” I opened the door.

“Nobody,” said Grandma. “Don’t stand there half naked. Go get dressed.”

They did come back late next evening.

The moon was already setting when I woke up to the barking of the neighbour’s dog, the creak of the gate. The muffled conversation in the kitchen made me crawl out of bed and glue an ear to the door, but I only could make out snatches of voices.

“Don’t rub too hard.”

“The bastard.”

“It stopped bleeding.”

“It’s swelling.”

“I’ll be all right.”

“You should’ve seen them,” that was Aunt Tera’s voice. “Staggering, dirty.”

"Starved," that was Anyu.

"He wept when I gave him that apple. That old man with that young boy dragging him along."

"He wasn't that old. Just exhausted. They couldn't stop even…"

"That's when he hit you," interrupted Aunt Tera.

"What is a bloody nose compared to…"

"He called you a whore. He could have pushed you into the line. You could be marching with them…"

"Maybe I should be…" cried Anyu.

"Your place is with your daughter."

I crawled back into bed.

The next night they were off again. Anyu with a black eye and swollen nose, Aunt Tera in her black boots and shawl.

They stopped whispering. Now it was their unspoken routine. I stopped asking questions.

Grandma took over the daily milking so that Aunt and Anyu could get some sleep in the morning.

Nothing surprised me any more. Not the dogfights in the sky, not the burning cities that lit up the horizon at night, not the homebound bombers that dropped their leftover bombs on empty fields.

I listened to the village drummer coming around the corner.

Tat-tat-tat----ta-tat, / Tat-tat-tat----ta-tat.

Everyone hurried out to the street, old men, women, children.

We waited in silence.

The old drummer shifted his drum to his side, unfolded a paper and announced in a faltering voice that we must greet each other from now on with the raised arm of a Hitler salute, not with a "good day".

Yet another order that everyone in the village ignored.

97

Bread for the doomed

They kept going night after night carrying apples and bread in their baskets. They trudged in the rain along country byways under tall poplars, across muddy creeks. They headed for a junction at a bend in the road where the endless procession of the doomed was driven towards the Austrian border.

They squatted behind bushes waiting for the right moment, when the guards turned the other way, to jump out and hand hunks of bread to the starving.

I didn't know where they went, where the bend in the road was where they were hiding because they wanted to spare me from knowing.

98

Through a bus window

It was 60 years after 1944, when I was 71, that I was shown that bend in the road. The ditch. The bushes. By then they were not the same bushes, not the same unpaved roads.

Can we pave over memories? Some say we can. But one day the new pavement will also vanish under weeds.

By the beginning of the 21st century one hardly could see a horse-drawn carriage, let alone cows on the roads. Only cars, buses, trucks and bicycles travelled between Püski and Mosonmagyaróvár. The morning bus departed the village filled with workers and students heading to the city and left Püski empty of the young, who returned to the village in the evening tired and weary.

I was back in the country visiting cemeteries and the few relatives and childhood friends who were still alive.

Terike took me back to Püski.

The bus was slow, so I had plenty of time to pester her with my usual questions about the past.

“Do you remember the nights we stripped the maize? Remember the songs we sang?”

“What was the name of the next door neighbour whose wife never said a word?

“When did Pajtás, the black dog die?”

She knew half the people in the crowded bus, something I grew accustomed to whenever I ventured with her anywhere in the county.

Having served as the local notary, often marrying those whose birth she earlier registered, filling out death and birth certificates, she played a role in so many lives at major turning points, a role she performed with compassion and good humour, it was no wonder that people were glad to greet her.

Across from us, sitting in the aisle seat, a young woman holding a child on her lap leaned over to tell her that her husband had gone to work in Hamburg and was sending home good money, but she missed him terribly. "He promised to come home for Christmas."

"How is your Grandma Varga? Terike asked.

"Oh, she passed on last winter."

"She was two years ahead of me in school."

"Mother is still alive. I'll tell her I met you. She's well, other than her arthritis."

When the baby started to cry, Terike turned back towards me and looked out the window.

"I'll show you something," she said. "Pay attention to the side of the road."

The old bus rolled on at a steady pace that was slow enough for me to observe the scrub thriving under the roadside poplars and the freshly-plowed land darkly stretching into the distance.

At an intersection the driver applied the brake to make a cautious left turn, and Terike pointed at the clump of trees and bushes on the corner.

"Look! That's the place."

"What?"

"The hiding place."

"You mean…"

"I mean that was the thicket where my mother and your mother lay hidden looking for your father among the people herded towards…"

"So you knew all along?"

"Mother showed it to me."

"Why didn't you show it to me then?

"Maybe…"

"Maybe what?"

"After you had gone to America, maybe you wanted to erase the memory of those days in 1944. Many of them do."

99

Apu's escapes

While I was feeding chickens and Anyu and Aunt Tera were squatting behind bushes by the road and scanning the faces of the doomed for my father, he was engaged in various ways of escape.

*

What I heard about his escapes during the cold days when we were hiding him at home made me tense and fearful.

I became confused by the conflicting expectations of adults. Why was Mr Bauer, my best friend Vica's father, so dangerous for Apu? Why did he want the Germans to win the war?

And if what I had heard was true, and they punished those Aryans who hid Jews, why did Apu choose mother and me to hide him?

One of the stories he told Anyu, the one I overheard one night when they thought I was asleep, the one I could never forget, was about a couple like them, arrested and tortured. For years in my nightmares I saw them being ordered to strip naked and copulate in front of the men who surrounded them laughing. I had no clear idea of what copulate meant, but I knew that it had to be an extreme act of violence.

Sometimes I wanted to hug Apu, to ask him to talk to me and not only to Anyu when he thought that I was asleep. To tell me all the details he knew, say those words that I missed when he whispered into her ear. I wanted to know every twist and turn of his many escapes.

I never got around to ask him. Instead, I made up a continuous narrative based on the little that I had heard. In my eyes, he turned into a reincarnation of Baron Münchhausen dodging danger with invincible wit, a shining "John the Valiant", a knight in tennis whites.

The way he crawled in Cservenka from brick kiln to kiln on a dark night while machineguns rattled by the ditches, slaughtering his mates, made me bury my face in my pillow.

When he described the march from Cservenka to Baja, he said that he could keep going when others fell by the wayside, were shot and kicked into roadside ditches, only because he had played tennis for years, while the others, weak city dwellers who sat all day at a desk, did not keep fit enough.

He said that he tried to stay away from the edges of the five-man rows, because those on the edges were often beaten, and that he stayed at the front, not in the back of the battalion, because the stragglers were shot.

What about me? I asked myself. Could I keep up, could I stay in the middle?

When they arrived at Pandúr Island, Hungarian soldiers and the good citizens of Baja brought them food, and they could drink water and bathe at last in the Danube. He managed to send a message to a bank president he knew in the city, having interviewed him in his

old reporter days. He asked for a change of clothes because he wore dirty rags by then. The bank president borrowed the uniform of the bank's doorman, a bright blue suit covered with gold braid and buttons together with a cap befitting a general and a pair of shoes so big, he said, they could have been props for a Charlie Chaplin movie.

Apu told me how he changed into this spectacular outfit behind a bush and, his head held high, how he walked across the bridge leading into town, smiling on the way and saluting the guards, who smiled back and waved as he passed.

Could I keep calm and collected? Or would I break into a run?

When he arrived in the bank, he was offered more fitting and less conspicuous clothes, "...clean underwear... and I was questioned by the bankers and remember the shocked faces when I told them about Cservenka," he said.

Bathed, shaved and relatively elegant, he boarded a train to Budapest.

On a street in Buda, he was stopped for an identity check by two teenagers wearing the dreaded Arrow Cross armbands and carrying machine guns. They arrested him.

He ended up in the Little Majestic Hotel, a newly designated prison, on the Sváb Mountain. About 40 prisoners were crammed into one room, waiting for interrogations that entailed beatings. He could hear the screams as he sat on the floor waiting for his turn, he said.

Someone came in and asked for a volunteer to work in the cellar. Nobody else volunteered, but he put up his hand.

He was led away to shovel coal in the basement, and felt relieved to get out of that crowded room. After a while, when the workman in charge of feeding the furnace stepped outside, he took one of the overalls covered with coal dust hanging on a nail, put it on, grabbed a shovel, climbed through a window and calmly walked away, waving to the guards outside. Don't ever run, he said. Walk at a leisurely pace.

He was looking for Ómama, and found her in a "Jewish house" on Szent István Körút. She fed him, and wanted to know everything. They talked into the night and fell asleep only to wake to a loud banging on the door. They tracked him down. This time they took him to the Mirabelle, a Gestapo prison.

His next stop was a cell at the Mária Terézia Barrack equipped with comfortable straw pallets, he said, and after five days, Christians were separated and sent to the front and Jews were taken to the Aréna Street Synagogue. Soldiers guarded the entrance and the crowd inside was desperate.

"I have decided to escape again," he said. He asked some of the others to go with him, but they were afraid to move and get shot by the guards. Seeing a small door in the back that seemed unguarded, he sneaked out into the night, climbed a fence and took off towards Fóti Road when the guards on the street were lighting a cigarette and looked the other way.

Where to go?

As he ran through a list of uncertain possibilities, he remembered an old friend. He was Dr Baron Attila Schroeder.

"A shy philosopher, author of *"The epistemological importance of dreams"*, the baron was a man of meagre means whose only source of income was piano playing in bars", Apu wrote later in his half-finished memoir. "His ancestors' castle was somewhere near Hannover. He was an old friend of mine. I respected his humanism and I knew that he often helped the persecuted."

The baron hid him in a neighbour's empty apartment, where he was told not to walk around on the creaky parquet floor, not to use the toilet or go to the window in order to avoid detection by other neighbours. After a week there, the owner, an army officer, wrote to the baron that he was soon due to leave the Russian front. Apu had to move. He asked the baron to send a coded telegram to us in Püski saying: *"Urgently find the Epistemology of Dreams".*

Mother understood that he was with the baron and that he needed her urgently. She decided to leave Püski. Grandma insisted on going with her and so did I. We packed up to get on the last train to enter from the west into besieged Budapest ringed by the Red Army.

It was not an easy voyage.

Aunt Tera had loaded us down with food to take: bags of flour, a sack of dried peas, a big blue bin filled with bits of fried goose buried in goose fat. She wrapped the bin in a thick towel and stuffed it in a backpack I had to carry. Anyu and Grandma carried the rest. If I bent forward far enough, the bin stayed on without much trouble.

Until it was time to board the train.

By the time we got to the station, sitting on a slow cart pulled by an old horse, the train was full and ready to leave. People hung on the steps and perched on the roofs of the carriages. Grandma and Anyu frantically looked around for a space, and I tried to keep up with them in the milling crowd. As I passed a puffing locomotive, I stumbled and, pulled back by the weight, sat down. I closed my eyes and started to feel hot.

A man yelled at me and lifted me up before my coat started to burn. I was sitting on a pile of hot ashes dumped on the side, but hung onto the bin. The man, whose name I never heard, carried me to an open window filled with people leaning out and handed me to another man who grabbed me and dragged me inside. Anyu and Grandma who saw this pushed themselves onto the steps of the same carriage and wormed themselves inside. Anyu was sobbing by the time she reached me.

We were standing all the way to Budapest, but I could lean on my bin held up by bodies pressing against me.

As soon as we arrived at home and put down our bags, Anyu was off in search of Apu and the baron.

Dodging German and Hungarian soldiers during a citywide curfew, she picked up Apu in the night. She had talked to Mr Kelemen before, who promised to leave the gate open for her on condition that he knew nothing.

Father was skin and bone and exhausted. He had to stay away from windows again, and couldn't flush the toilet during air raids while we were down in the shelter, but by then he was used to being a fugitive.

With much of our furniture left in Püski, Anyu managed to borrow beds, and we settled into the routine of air raids at night and hours of lull during the day, when the noise of cannons coming closer made us think that one day all this must be over.

100

Coming to grips with Bor

I must admit that for many years after the war I didn't want to read or think about 1944.

Bor and Cservenka were too dark, too harrowing chapters.

Pretending not to know was easier than carrying the weight of knowing.

I clung to Apu's jokey details about friendly crickets chirping in the cracks of his hut in Bor and about the love letters he was ordered to pen for illiterate sergeants.

It was only now, in old age that finally I wanted to know more.

To learn about the history of the forced labour camp in Bor, I turned to a book published in 2011 by Tamás Csapody in Budapest: *The forced labourers of Bor.*

After years of meticulous research and interviews with survivors, he presented a comprehensive picture of the times and conditions in this study. He supplied a list of the copious source materials he had read, and he gave nearly all of the names of the men who perished and those who stayed alive.

With his permission, I quote from a few of his publications.

*

On 20 November 1940 Hungary joined the Tripartite Pact with Germany, Italy and Japan.

On 6 April 1941 Germany attacked Yugoslavia, and so did Regent Miklós Horthy and the government of László Bárdossy a few days later. Hungarian soldiers occupied the Yugoslavian region of Bačka. A few months later, on 26 June, Hungary declared war on the Soviet Union.

Under the Horthy regime the first labour service law was brought into effect in March 1939. The aim was to gather all politically unreliable individuals, and use their manpower for military purposes. Labour service enlistees mainly included communists, people belonging to various ethnicities, as well as Romas and Jews.

Treatment of these servicemen got worse and worse, and labour service had an increasingly punitive character. By the beginning of 1943 the number of labour servicemen reached 50,000.

In the German-occupied territory of Yugoslavia Germany took possession of the mines and industrial facilities, too, including the

very important (formerly French-owned) Bor mining region. This region in southeast Serbia (in the Serbian Ore Mountains close to the Romanian and Bulgarian borders) had valuable raw materials for the production of weaponry (copper, nickel, tin and lead). From 1942 these mines provided fifty percent of Germany's total ore requirement for its war efforts.

For mining and processing, as well as for the increase of production, the Germans required more and more workers. To this end, they decided on the use of forced labour. Therefore, from the end of 1942 until the autumn of 1944 a labour camp complex employing 30,000 to 80,000 forced labourers was organised in Bor and its vicinity.

In addition to "Yugoslavs" living on the territory of Yugoslavia (Bosniaks, Croats, Hungarians, Serbs, Slovenes, Jews), captured partisans, Czech, French, Greek, Polish and Romanian workers, as well as a large number of Italian prisoners of war (following Italy's withdrawal from the war in May 1943), were living and toiling in the region.

Work was directed by Organisation Todt (OT), the German military labour organisation with the German Siemens factory providing the professional background. Therefore, the forced labourers became Siemens employees.

As much as 98 per cent of the labour servicemen sent to Yugoslavia by Hungary in 1943 were Jewish. The remaining two per cent, around 200 people, were members of minority churches.

Germany invaded Hungary on 19 March 1944. The Germans demanded that more and more forced labourers be sent to Bor from Hungary. The government now no longer hesitated to fulfill the request, and it provided the Germans with 3,000 Jewish labour servicemen under the same conditions.

The labour servicemen arrived in Bor in the summer of 1944 and were placed at the seven subsidiary labour camps situated to the north-west of Bor, and were made to construct a narrow-gauge railway over the mountains.

My father was part of this group.

Many of the 6,000 labour servicemen taken to Bor were well known figures from the world of culture, arts, public life or politics, including the internationally known great Hungarian poet, Miklós Radnóti, and the poet László Lukács, who died in Bor. The well-known Social Democratic politician, Pál Justus was one of the older servicemen. All three of them served in Bor under the command of Lieutenant Colonel Ede Marányi. During Marányi's tenure the cruel forms of punishment, torture and executions were used on a massive scale.

On 23 August 1944 Romania pulled out of the war, as a result of which the Soviets quickly forced the German troops to retreat from the Balkans. The Hungarian Ministry of Defence called the Hungarian soldiers and labour servicemen back from Bor.

The first group of labour servicemen left Bor on 17 September 1944. The greatest losses were incurred at Crvenka in the West Bačka region of Serbia. Here German soldiers, with the support of Hungarian soldiers, executed 800 to 1,000 Jewish labour servicemen during the night of 7 October 1944.

*

My father did not die in Cservenka. He kept going.

The following are his own words translated by me from Hungarian.

"Marching from Cservenka to Baja, you needed stamina. Men younger than me could not keep going. I tried to stay in the middle of the pack, look ahead, breathe to a rhythm. Those who were doing sedentary work all their lives, accountants, lawyers, bankers, tailors fared worse than physical workers, farmers, builders and mechanics.

"Thoughts were also important. I hung unto the future. I wanted to believe in the future. I said to my friend marching next to me, think of your wife. She is waiting for you. Walk towards her. She is handing you a slice of bread. Walk towards the bread.

"We were starving.

"He ran off the road as we passed a beet field to pull up some roots and eat. He was shot.

"I kept going, breathing to a rhythm."

The following prose-poem is about this march. I had to write it a few years ago:

how to master marching orders

when the call sounds - fall in - line up - best to stay calm and act fast feigning obedience - try to secure a place up front not in the back of the column - the second row in the middle is your best bet that way you are less visible than the first row but still leading not slowing down as the last rows are apt to provoke curses blows with gun butts and reprisals - try to stay as nondescript and obliging as you can to please the guards who do not like men who look awkward truculent and make their job unpleasant - if the order is to sing a jolly song give it a go wholeheartedly if you can - it may help to step in rhythm if your feet are buckling - don't react to demeaning words curses nor to ridicule - stick to your old dignity - think of mother - wife or daughter - think of days of spring blossoms but don't ever take your eyes off what's ahead never look back at the straggling ragtag ranks for if you trip stumble and fall it is hard to rise again before a kick lands on your back or your head and if you can't get to your feet a quick bullet into your skull may end it all - be sure not to volunteer for shovel duty to cover the carcasses for the ground is hard to dig up on the run - you tire fast and soon you are too weary to carry on – then may collapse under a tree throw your shovel in the ditch turn to the sky to see the clouds passing by and wait for the flash of a gun

Lessons learned from my father

he showed mother
the hole in his hip
said it was made
with the butt of a gun

I heard him talk
about ditches dug
about sliding over bodies
in squelching mud
of clay and blood
while up-up above
a lethal line
of smoking guns
was loaded again
and again
by cursing men

he talked about
tangles of trampled grass
and how his breath
melted the ice
on frozen windows
in abandoned rooms

he taught me
how to stay alive
how to lie
to hide
to smile
and above all
to wait until
the Devil's fall.

101

Hitler's orders

Attack! Fight unto death!

No more withdrawals!

Keep the Soviet hordes from reaching Vienna!

Hitler was adamant. He turned Hungary into a bloody battlefield.

The Soviet army was closing its ring around Budapest, and the war soon reached the village we left behind.

It arrived with an exhausted SS officer retreating from the Russian front, but still putting on an impeccably elegant front. He took over the only room. His elderly orderly, who had to sleep in the kitchen and polish his boots and iron out the creases of his uniform every day, told Aunt Tera that he wished he was back at home in Bavaria milking cows again.

The artillery fire boomed closer, and the SS soon vanished.

The Russians arrived. As they searched through every house and entered the room, they took note of our fancy bed and the varnished wardrobe and became suspicious.

"Burzsuj", they shouted at Uncle Pista pointing at the city furniture, meaning "rich man, class enemy".

Luckily, he had learned enough Russian in the First World War and could explain that he did not own the furniture. Aunt Tera's offer of her last duck eggs in a basket further smoothed the ruffled mood and lifted the spirit of the soldiers who took the eggs plus two hens and carried on.

102

Flaming blackouts

Budapest was a harder nut to crack for the Russians.

During the long siege candles were worth their weight in gold.

We couldn't go shopping when no shops were open any more. The streets were abandoned. Even earlier, when some brave shop owners still rolled up their roller shutters, and bullets didn't ricochet on the sidewalks, shelves were empty of candles, sold out at the start of the bombing.

I could go down the whole alphabet to list all the goods regularly out of stock.

That's when I learned to make candles.

Vica and I would sit together in the shelter on the edge of her horsehair mattress with a *hokedli* planted in front of us. We were kneading balls of half-melted, soft paraffin on plates, re-using candle-drips to make new candles, using shoelaces for wicks. We were proud of our handiwork as we watched our mothers strike a match to light up our gnarled and soot-stained creations.

Candles seemed to me alive.

Their flame reacted to our breath and moved when someone passed by. They fed on their paraffin-soaked wick as they visibly ate up themselves.

I could watch for a long time a candle dance and flare. I loved the smell of its angry smoke when its wick got too long and curled up under its own weight.

The way it illuminated faces showed a talent for exaggeration. Someone like Vica with her smooth child face close to a flame looked like a puffy angel. Someone like her grandfather looked like a rigid woodcarving made with a heavy hand. Her father's mouth seemed set in stone under his moustache. All this was less evident whenever the electric bulb overhead lit up again.

Sometimes the sirens started too late. By the time they began to wail, we were already wide awake, startled by the roar of planes overhead. We began our weary descent on the staircase, lugging whatever we had stacked up by the door.

In spite of Anyu urging me to hurry up, I often stopped halfway on the stairs to watch the intense beams of light rapidly scanning the black sky and zeroing in on the bombers. Soon more than one converged on a victim followed by a spray of bullets aimed at the moving target that was attempting to change course and rise above their trajectory.

This high drama was played out against a dark stage under the glare of spotlights directing my eyes to the centre of action. I could stand and watch the fireworks forever, but Anyu would grab my arm and drag me down the stairs.

And there were the fires. The brilliance of flames lit by incendiary bombs. Not only by those. Ordinary bombs could start a fire as well, if they ruptured a gas pipe or tipped over a potbelly stove. When we emerged from the cellars, burning buildings lit up the night, sent flames leaping from roof to roof, created the bonfires of war. They left their sooty mementos, rubble and the stench of damp mortar, of smoky ashes. I avoided those, didn't linger among blackened bricks and bric-a-brac. I preferred the drama of the flames, their roar, their urgency, the taste of danger, not its aftermath.

103

O, du lieber Augustin

O, du lieber Augustin, Augustin, Augustin
Alles ist hin.
Debrecin
Szegedin
Alles ist hin.

When did I learn this song?

Was it on a propaganda leaflet dropped by a Soviet or an American plane that fluttered to a halt on the snow-covered factory yard? Or was it a song I heard on the radio that broke through the officially crackling barriers meant to smother Radio Free Europe?

Or was it broadcast by loudspeakers towards Buda Castle by Russian intelligence officers trying to convince the besieged SS and Hungarian troops that there was no point in fighting any longer? Did the music stream over the Danube during those few nights when the guns took a momentary rest? I am not sure.

I didn't know then that the song was born during the bubonic plague, that it was a beloved German tune, but I knew what it meant, what the two city names: Debrecin, Szegedin, meant. The song told us that the Russians have taken the two cities of Debrecen and Szeged, that they were unstoppable, that they pushed back the Germans from Moscow all the way to Budapest.

I could hum it. I could whistle it without retribution. After all, it was an old German folk song.

I have learned enough German in kindergarten to know what it meant. Dear Augustin, all is lost. All is lost dear Augustin.

I didn't need Apu to translate it for me.

104

Fear

Fear starts in the legs, rushes up the thighs, tightens the abdomen, stabs the heart and holds in the breath. When the roar of the planes recedes, it slackens its grip, but lies in wait for the next jolt.

No man's land

These words address
the fate of the unnamed many
who were summarily
shot or hanged

Teenagers and married fathers
mama's boys and virgin sweethearts
volunteered or conscripted
sent off with songs
hugs and kisses
to end up in no man's land
ducking under hissing missiles
and bullets.

Crawling
climbing

pissing
charging
seeing dying mates ahead
if in panic turned
and buried their head in dread,
they were called
cowards.

Firing squads
picked from comrades
pulled the triggers on command
watched them crumple
stripped of honour
buried in a blood-drenched land.

105

István Kaszap's fire

It wasn't about clinging to a straw of hope. It was more solid than that.

I was clinging to an unbreakable, unfrayable robust rope directly tied to heaven when I asked young István Kaszap to save us.

Please, intervene on our behalf! Please, tell God to send them away! To drop their bombs somewhere else! Blessed István pray for us! Amen.

I never heard of him, until…

It was our Chin-Chin Hen-in-Pants teacher (the kindly nun we were fond of and whose freckled face still appears on my retina whenever I think of her) who introduced us to István Kaszap. She told us not to be afraid. Trust in God to look after us, the way István Kaszap trusted our Heavenly Father in the midst of his suffering. She compared him to Job, the suffering innocent.

A bunch of 10- and 11-year-old girls in school, quite content to miss a dull class in favour of an air raid drill, we were sitting on benches lined up against the walls, shivering in the freshly whitewashed shelter of the school, when she handed out a leaflet small enough to fit into my ivory-white prayer book. On one side it had the photo of a handsome young man of kindly but serious demeanor. A short summary of his life was printed under the picture, letting us know that he was 19 when he died, but in spite of the limited time allowed, he lived a rich and meaningful life dedicated to service on his way to priesthood, his unfulfilled dream.

Our tall nun's voice shrank almost to a whisper when she told us that young István had endured with superhuman piety the immense suffering visited upon him by God in order to test his faith. During the last year of his life in spite of excruciating pain and debilitating fever, he offered his prayers for those who had greater burdens to bear than his own. She told us that his prayers have often been answered, and many of those for whom he had interceded testified that their circumstances improved and that they were saved.

Ignis sacer, (she spelled it out for us) a disease called "sacred fire" (also called sometimes St Anthony's Fire), engulfed István Kaszap, plunging him into all-consuming fevers alternating with chills, and terrible boils that suppurated all over his body, the infection spreading into the deeper tissues. She described the festering wounds adding that there was no medicine to help him and because his throat swelled and he could not breathe or swallow they had to cut a hole in his neck.

He will be a saint one day, she said, because during his short life he already was heard by God and could perform miracles. That is why Székesfehérvár, his hometown has been spared and never been bombed.

"Take this prayer and keep it on you," she advised. "Recite it during air raids, and no bomb will fall upon you. He will intercede on your behalf, if you humbly ask him for his help."

I read it to Grandma, and she agreed that it might help. I didn't show it to Anyu and Apu, because I knew that they wouldn't understand. During the long siege, I often recited this request crouching on my stool in the shelter whenever the detonations came too close. In my prayer I always included my parents and Grandma and Ómana.

I could not imagine myself being covered by running sores like István Kaszap, but I could attempt to pray as often as he did, and maybe, I thought, I should enter a nunnery after the war and spend my life in God's service to thank Him and become worthy of His attention.

We didn't suffer a direct hit, that's for sure. But after the war, we were so busy with searching for food, fuel and for lost friends and relatives, that I never thanked István Kaszap. For a while I even forgot about him, until my university colleague, Mária moved in with us in 1953 and told us about the terrible damage inflicted upon the people of his Székesfehérvár in the final phase of the war.

sleeping bombs

there is a bomb
in the garden

it landed
with a thump
raised a cloud
of grey dust

we keep doors
tightly closed
afraid that it
may explode

our two hens
are alone
in the garden
can't go out
to feed them

I must pray
that the hens
don't go near
to wake up
the dud bomb

we only have
those two hens
but there are
plenty of
sleeping bombs

106

Beautiful shrapnel

I kept my collection in a pouch, which I kept under my mattress. It was exciting to search for shrapnel after the first air raids, when they were still a novelty. These bits of misshapen metal resembled cut-offs from the workshop of a mad toolmaker. The sharp edges could slice my fingers. Their weight was substantial. They looked like miniature dragons, crippled Minotaurs, porcupines and snakes.

My friend, Vica, and I were engaged in a collecting competition that appeared to be more to her advantage.

I figured it out eventually that her father, Mr Bauer was helping her. As the commander of the shelter, he was in-and-out all the time even during air raids, when we were strictly forbidden to go out. That way he had the chance to get the biggest and most interesting fragments before I could lay an eye on them. Vica and I used to trade them. She generously let me have a bigger one for two of mine.

After the war I forgot about them and started collecting stamps. I don't remember what happened to my lethal collection. Maybe I dumped them or traded them for a pretty French stamp. Or a rare Portuguese.

107

My war poem

One afternoon I wrote a poem.

I was fond of verses that chimed at the end of each line, the rhymes suggesting a reassuring order. It could be that this was my way of subduing the surrounding chaos with rhythmic hammer blows of sound pounding at regular intervals. My rhymes were rooted in the nursery ditties and the rhyming proverbs of *Kisalföld* lore recited to me by Grandma ever since the day I was born.

My poem was harmless, but the refrain at the end of each stanza raised a question that could have met with the objections of our military masters engaged in "a life-death struggle" against the "Bolshevik hordes and their allies".

I only remember the refrain:

Why is there war when on
our beautiful planet
Snowbells rise from the snow
In each silent forest?

In Hungarian:

Miért is van háború
hisz oly szép a világ
a csendes erdőben
nyílik a hóvirág.

Was I also influenced by the Katalin Karády tune endlessly played on our wind-up gramophone during the war?

Everything draws to an end
Everything passes away
And every December
Heralds a new May.

Karády's deep, resonant voice, almost conversational, insinuated itself into the fabric of the blacked-out streets of Budapest, into our nights spent undrground, into the mood of an exhausted country.

It was the winter of injured, dormant gardens and icy, debris-filled sidewalks, shattered windows held together by sticky tape and cardboard, abandoned rooms and stifling cellars.

108

The horse

Old Kelemen told Grandma about the horse. She didn't hesitate for a moment. I watched her as she rushed around knocking on doors and telling about it to Paula and the wife of our new bombed-out neighbours who moved in after the Kendes were made to move to a Jewish house.

Pretty soon half the house was on the street joined by people from other houses coming armed with hatchets and knives to carve up the dead horse lying on the corner of Bulcsu Street. I was not allowed to go.

Grandma came back with slabs of half-frozen meat in our tin bucket and tipped them under the faucet. Some still had patches of brown hair attached mixed with ice and snow. I didn't look when she skinned and carved up the flesh to put it to boil on the stove. We had meat stew that night, and all agreed that it tasted all right, maybe a bit sweeter than beef, but it filled our stomach.

After dinner I went to the kitchen and lifted the lid of the rubbish box. Among some dry onion skins I found a piece of the hide and lifted it out holding it between my thumb and forefinger. It was shiny. And wet. The snow had melted.

Grandma ripped it out of my hand and threw it back banging the lid down. "It was a dead horse," she said pushing me out of the kitchen.

"In Paris during the famine they ate everything. Even rats," Apu said, and that made us feel better.

"Was this a German horse?" I asked Grandma.

"No. It was a Hungarian horse. One of the men cutting it up said its name. It was called Fickó."

"Fickó?"

"Yes. Fickó. There's enough stew left for tomorrow."

109

Mulberry memories

After an air raid, when we can leave the cellar and trudge back up the stairs, yawning in the grey morning light, trying to snatch a short sleep in real beds instead of huddling on chairs, I am too tired to eat.

Grandma insists that I swallow a ladleful of soup or, if I am lucky, some of the remaining noodles we brought back from Püski. Back in the village she still had the time to knead the dough, to roll it out on the kitchen table, cut it into fine strips and dry it outside, spread on a white cloth in the sun.

I like to imagine that the egg she used for those noodles is the one I found hidden in the bushes around the edge of the garden, the egg laid by a rogue hen in secret, preparing to brood. And what makes it taste even better is the thought that I am eating Uncle Pista's flour milled from the wheat he harvested the summer I carried his midday meal in the scorching sun from Aunt Tera's kitchen all the way to the far wheat fields.

Anyu tucks me in and tells me to get a wink of sleep, and I embark on my habitual dream voyage to Püski.

As I close my eyes, I am treading the dusty paths that meander among the acres of barley, oats and corn, paths lined with thistles, cornflowers and bright red poppies. I have a chance to submerge in the immensity of the fertile land called *Kisalföld.*

I ponder why it was named "Kisalföld", meaning "small lowland", when it seemed to me enormous, a plain dotted with church spires in the shimmering hazy distance? Then I remind myself that in school I learned that the name had to contrast with the even bigger Great Hungarian Plain.

It feels good to feel the pride of knowing. It relaxes my body as I stretch and roll over to my other side pulling my *dunyha* over my head.

Walking becomes easy now, unless I forget to pay attention to the path ahead. I must not stumble on the flattened patches of cow dung drying in the deep ruts made by ox-drawn carriages that belong to villagers much better off than my uncle, who only owns one milking cow. No carriage.

When I get hot and tired, I stop under an old mulberry tree, a favourite dwelling of silkworms. I carefully put down my food carrier, a heavy but ingenious contraption, made of a stack of three enameled pots threaded through by two metal strips with a handle on top.

Relishing the warmth of my bed, I force myself to recall every detail of that familiar food carrier, its weight, its handle, the way it bumps against my side.

It can keep the meat, the noodles, the soup, the boiled potatoes (anything my aunt cooks that day) hot until I arrive at my destination. My other hand holds a basket with bread or baked sweets wrapped in a cloth alongside apples or pears, peaches or apricots, whatever happens to be ripe and ready to eat.

Stopping in the shade for a few moments I gather some of the fallen mulberries spread as a purple blanket under the trees, still fresh on the soft grass which is thick in the shade, not like over the fields, dry and brittle already. I pick up a handful and savour their sweetness, getting their juice all over my hands and running down my chin, leaving telltale marks on my apron as well.

When I am even more relaxed and feel my toes getting warm, I attempt to take stock of all my aprons through the years, recalling every lace trim, every rickrack.

They have been made by both Grandma and Ómama. They are frothy white cotton for school and printed percale decorated with rickrack trim and flounces resting on my shoulders for tasks at home. Tied around my waist with a bow in the back, my aprons are the emblems of my usefulness.

Now I am getting closer to my destination. In the distance I can make out the silhouette of Uncle Pista and the glint of his scythe in the blazing sun. I stop under a tree and wait for the church bell to ring. They see me, but they don't stop until the bell tolls. I don't put down the food because of too many hungry ants.

Uncle Pista is swinging his scythe, the one he sharpened the night before. He sways to a steady rhythm that he doesn't vary from sunup to sundown, a rhythm that keeps him going even after he is worn out.

Terike follows him. She is bent low gathering and binding the sheaves, her red kerchief tight on her forehead, her apron askew.

Ferike hauls the sheaves into a stack closer to the road and sits down on the ground to pick out a prickle from his bare foot.

He grins at me, and I grin back but don't move.

I am not to help them. I am a city girl, I don't know how.

When they stop and settle on the grass verge, I join them and take a drink from the round-bellied unglazed pitcher that keeps the water deliciously cool by letting it slowly evaporate on its damp outside skin.

There is never a scrap of food left, and as I gather up the dishes to walk back to the village, I see Uncle Pista straighten his legs and lie down in the grass with his arms crossed under his head and his old hat pulled over his eyes to catch a short rest. Only his hand waves periodically, whenever a fly lands on his chin.

By and by, I am also ready to sleep in the midst of summer memories. Sleep, precious sleep comes to me of its own accord.

110

Present tense

No, I am not in Püski under a mulberry tree any longer.

Uncle Pista, Terike and Ferike are long dead.

I am an old woman now, standing in the Van Gogh Museum in Amsterdam looking at *The sheaf-binder* whose body rising from the turmoil of harvest is rooted in the landscape. In Van Gogh's painting, he works with the same intensity I observed as a child. He uses his knees, his elbows, his hands, his shoulders, his neck, every muscle and every sinew of his body to haul his dusty bundle.

I see in him my ancestors, the multitudes of those who went before me, engaged in the unending toil for food.

Take me back

(Hosanna for a small planet)

Take me back
to the stone-cobbled street
lined with lush acacias,
where the streetcar's squeal
mingled with the curses of men
as they whipped their heaving horses
until horseshoes sparked against the stones
where butchers spread sawdust on shop floors
dairies sold chocolate cows
and the old concierge
swept the sidewalk with slow strokes
where I learned to read and write
and how to pray and mourn

carry me
carry me home

To the two-room mud house
scented by rising damp
boiling corn and baking bread
where we drank from a communal mug
dipped into a bucket drawn
from a deep garden well
where cows slurped from a barrel
I was allowed to enter

on sweltering days
and watch the rooster mount a hen
among rattling leaves of horseradish
where if my ears rose above water
I could hear a far thresher drone,

carry me
carry me home

To the attic room on the corner
of Lake and Third near Presidio
where I walked through a golf course
on rainy days when eucalyptus
perfumed the air and I paused
among the headstones of soldiers
facing the arching promise of Golden Gate
to the corner where we embraced
with urgent young abandon

carry me
carry me home

To the fern-shaded house
we built in dense bush
among wind-sculpted kanuka
where moreporks kept watch
and the carnal fantail flirted
with all passers-by
where kingfishers' nests
were carved in clay banks
and we feasted on
bearded mussels and fat oysters
where sailboats sheltered
from many a storm

carry me
carry me home

Dare I go on?
To the quayside in Tahiti
to the ruins of Oaxaca
the shrouded peaks of Peru
humming markets of Mombasa
to the domains of my daydreams
calving icebergs on wind-swept poles
shifting dunes of dry Saharas
graying vaults of old cathedrals
crowded mosques
synagogues
ashrams and abandoned altars
to the flood plains of the Danube
on a white boat from the Black Sea
let me float by Parliament's dome

take me back
carry me home

111

Auntie Zita

Goebbels promised "wonder weapons" to the German people, making them believe that they still can win the war, while I stood by the gate watching old men bent over rucksacks and bags, women dragging tired toddlers by one hand and carrying blankets with the other, children pushing prams loaded with clothes and pillows, heads wrapped in scarves, eyes nailed to the ground. The procession was endless. It only stopped whenever the sirens sounded and a sleek German anti-aircraft gun, newly planted on the corner, started to boom.

Auntie Zita suddenly turned up after an "All Clear", when we were sitting around the table.

We heard a knock on the door. Apu rushed into the bathroom to climb out the airshaft window. Anyu shouted , "One moment, please," and followed him to help and throw the grey blanket to cover him when he landed. She had to remove the stool he used to reach the windowsill.

Grandma rose with deliberate slowness to open the door. She stood there without saying a word.

Anyu came back to look, and gasped. She recognized the figure standing there. My godmother, Auntie Zita.

Her head was wrapped in white gauze. Only her eyes, nose and mouth were free. She looked like a ghost, a specter with a huge white head that kept wobbling. She was bent under a dusty bundle she carried over her shoulder.

She said, "I am here," and leaned against the doorframe.

Anyu lifted off the bundle from her back and placed it on the floor. Grandma kicked it aside and helped her into a chair. As soon as she sat down, she started to sob.

Yes, Auntie Zita was my godmother.

It meant a lot to be a godmother then. When I was a child, there were more reasons to fear early death than now. God-motherhood was not only a religious convention, a vague "I promise, with God's help, to raise this orphan as a good Catholic". Parents needed to be assured that somebody would look after their children in case they died. They chose a close friend, a family they trusted for this role.

Auntie Zita and her husband Oszkár were such friends. Their background was similar to Anyu's and Apu's. Oszkár was Jewish and Zita was Roman Catholic. Oszkár was a writer like Apu, and Zita also had to work to support them both, like Anyu. She was a slender blonde beauty with a singsong laughter and dancing feet, who turned heads wherever she went.

Before the war, she was a carefree woman. Because our one-room apartment was of minimal size, all our socializing happened in coffee houses during leisurely Sunday afternoons. After a noon meal, we'd walk towards the Danube and settle at a table on a sunny sidewalk or, if it was windy or cold, inside a café around a marble-topped table to welcome friends and acquaintances. Oszkár and Zita were among them.

She and Anyu were the kind of close friends who rarely met. Aunt Zita worked in a famous salon downtown selling gowns to rich and titled women. That's why she was so well dressed and well groomed, while Anyu, who also liked to dress fashionably, couldn't afford that sort of elegance.

Imagine our shock seeing her head wrapped in gauze, stained and dusty, her body bundled in a coat that was torn and equally dirty.

She sat there crying.

Apu appeared dragging the grey blanket on the floor and stood there silently.

"Get these off," Anyu ordered, pulling off her coat and handing her a handkerchief.

"I climbed out," said Aunt Zita still crying, her voice mixed with sudden hiccups.

"Climbed out," Anyu repeated. "Out of what?"

"The crater, I was buried. Deep. In the crater. A direct hit. Next to me a hand. It was my neighbour's. The old lawyer. It didn't move. When I woke up under the rubble. The bricks. His hand."

"First you must rest and eat," said Anyu. "Tell us later."

"I had a door over me. I could still breathe. The hand. But he was under the bricks. Dead. I couldn't see his head. The door saved me."

I moved closer to her to hear. She pulled me even closer and held my hand.

"I was alive," she said. "The only one left alive."

"Your head," Grandma started, but Auntie Zita ignored her.

"There was silence. No one else moved. I tried to shift some bricks in front of my face, but my feet were stuck and I had blood in my eyes. I had to wipe my face. I heard the voice of a man who came looking. He lifted the door and dug me out. He carried me to a place where they gave me aspirin and washed my head. They wrapped it up and sent me home."

"Home?" Apu put the grey blanket over her knees.

"Home?" Aunt Zita repeated in almost a whisper. "My home is in the crater under that door."

"I am glad you came to us," Anyu said.

"I couldn't find much when I went back there to look for my things. But you might be able to use some of this, " she pointed at the bundle she brought.

Grandma lifted it up and placed it on the table. She turned it around and struggled to unknot the soiled pillowcase. It contained a damp pillow, a curled up tube of toothpaste, a single shoe that was obviously a man's, a dirty tennis ball, a chipped glass vase and a few books, one of which was a small book of poems by Villon, torn, but still readable.

That's how I met Villon at age eleven.

112

A hot bath for Auntie Zita

The big air raid that buried my godmother interrupted the gas supply for a time. Fortunately, it was restored by the time she arrived at our door, and Anyu could help her take off her dusty and torn clothes, while Grandma filled the tub with warm water for a restorative soak. She got into the tub with Anyu's assistance and fell into a deep sleep that lasted until the bathwater turned cold.

It was a renewed Auntie Zita who emerged dressed in one of Anyu's *kombinés* topped by her quilted robe. Only the gauze covering her skull remained dirty. She didn't let anyone touch her head.

Without waiting for supper, which was plain *köménymag* soup and dry yellow peas, she fell asleep again on my *sezlony* relegating me to share the bed with my parents. I tucked Villon under my pillow, and instead of my usual evening prayer, kept repeating his line: 'In my own country, I am in a far off land'.

It was the not first time that something made me feel that I was stuck in the wrong place, that I should be in some other room, in another city, another continent. My eyes wouldn't close, and I shivered with an unaccountable expectation. I snuggled closer to Anyu and couldn't help thinking about the possibility of being buried in rubble with a dead hand for company.

Luckily, Anyu's body was warm and I could feel her breathing with a regular rhythm in and out, in and out. Apu's stentorian snoring also helped me return to the present, to the adults asleep in the room.

That night the sirens didn't start up until it was almost dawn. We were slow to get down into the shelter because Auntie Zita didn't want to go. Grandma, emerging from her kitchen cot, had to force her to put on the robe and wrap a blanket over her shoulders. She was whimpering and stopped half way down in the stairwell until Anyu pushed and Grandma grabbed her hand to drag her. She was still whimpering when Bauer closed the hermetic door behind us. All of us sat silently listening to the roaring planes and the thumping anti-aircraft guns.

When the bombs started to fall, her voice changed, she started to shout, "No, no, no!" then she let out an inarticulate squeal, and her breathing gathered speed with gulps and higher and higher screams.

Everyone was looking at her, a white-gauzed ghost head over a grey blanket. Everyone was motionless. Then Mr Bauer rose from his chair and walked up to her. "Shut up!" he ordered.

She couldn't stop, and he bent down and slapped her. Her head pivoted, and she moaned before she fell silent.

"We can't allow hysteria," shouted Bauer loud enough for everyone to hear over the racket outside.

Anyu pulled her chair closer to her own and embraced and rocked Auntie Zita, who kept wiping the area of her nose with a corner of her blanket.

She stayed with us for a few days, until she made up her mind to go. She said she wanted to look for her mother somewhere near Csepel. There was no way to hold her back. Grandma wrapped up a few patties of the fried peas to take for the road.

This was the way then. People turned up only to disappear suddenly.

When I met her husband, Oscar, 50 years later in Budapest, he was living in a ground floor flat in Pozsonyi Street with another wife and told me that Zita died not long after the war. "She never recovered a hundred per cent."

I didn't ask him for details while his second wife, a smiling old woman, stood behind his chair resting a hand on his shoulder and listening to our every word. I thanked him instead for writing a generous obituary about my father, his old colleague.

113

Sandbagged dreams

In 1944, I thought that being afraid was natural. I sensed that my fear was shared by everyone all around me. It was the unacknowledged mindset of the world. Fear was the air we breathed, and we didn't talk about it.

In the bomb shelter I tried to be brave, not to show naked terror like Aunt Zita. I didn't want to be slapped. Even in the worst moments I tried not to scream, not to disgrace myself.

But nightmares don't lie. They let us know what we don't want to know.

One of my recurring nightmares to this day involves a crippling hesitation.

Which door should I choose? Which gate should I bang on? Which staircase should I run down when the bombs start to fall?

I find myself close to a railroad station, or an army barrack, an anti-aircraft battery, or anything else considered a target. Terrified, I start my dream run to get as far as possible from the approaching planes. I keep trying to duck down into solidly built apartment houses seeking shelter in well-sandbagged cellars.

In my dream all gates are locked in front of me. They do this as protection against thieves who could use an air raid to loot empty apartments. The reinforced doors of the shelters are also shut to keep out air blasts as well as casual passers-by from the street. Too many extra bodies could use up the limited oxygen too fast in a sealed cellar.

The sirens keep wailing in my head in waves of rising and falling notes. I panic in neighbourhoods I don't recognize. As in a *film noir*, the streets are gritty grey, the sky dark, the planes throb, the pavement trembles, and I keep running.

The Bridges of Budapest

They span the Danube
a river that's never blue
but brown when it floods
red when it's stained
with the blood
of innocents
and dirty grey
when slabs of ice
turn into soiled chunks
piling up at their stone feet

a determined rushing
rolling
restless and
never slowing
river
flowing
from the Black Forest
to the Black Sea
from black to black

melancholy river
savage river
washes the feet
of the bridges of Budapest.

The winter of 1944

Last night
the frost crept close,
locked its jaw over the house
and left crystal wreaths
of its acid breath
etched on the windows.

Thick ice welded
the front door to its frame.

We had to wield a hatchet
to get out,
to shatter this glacial paralysis.

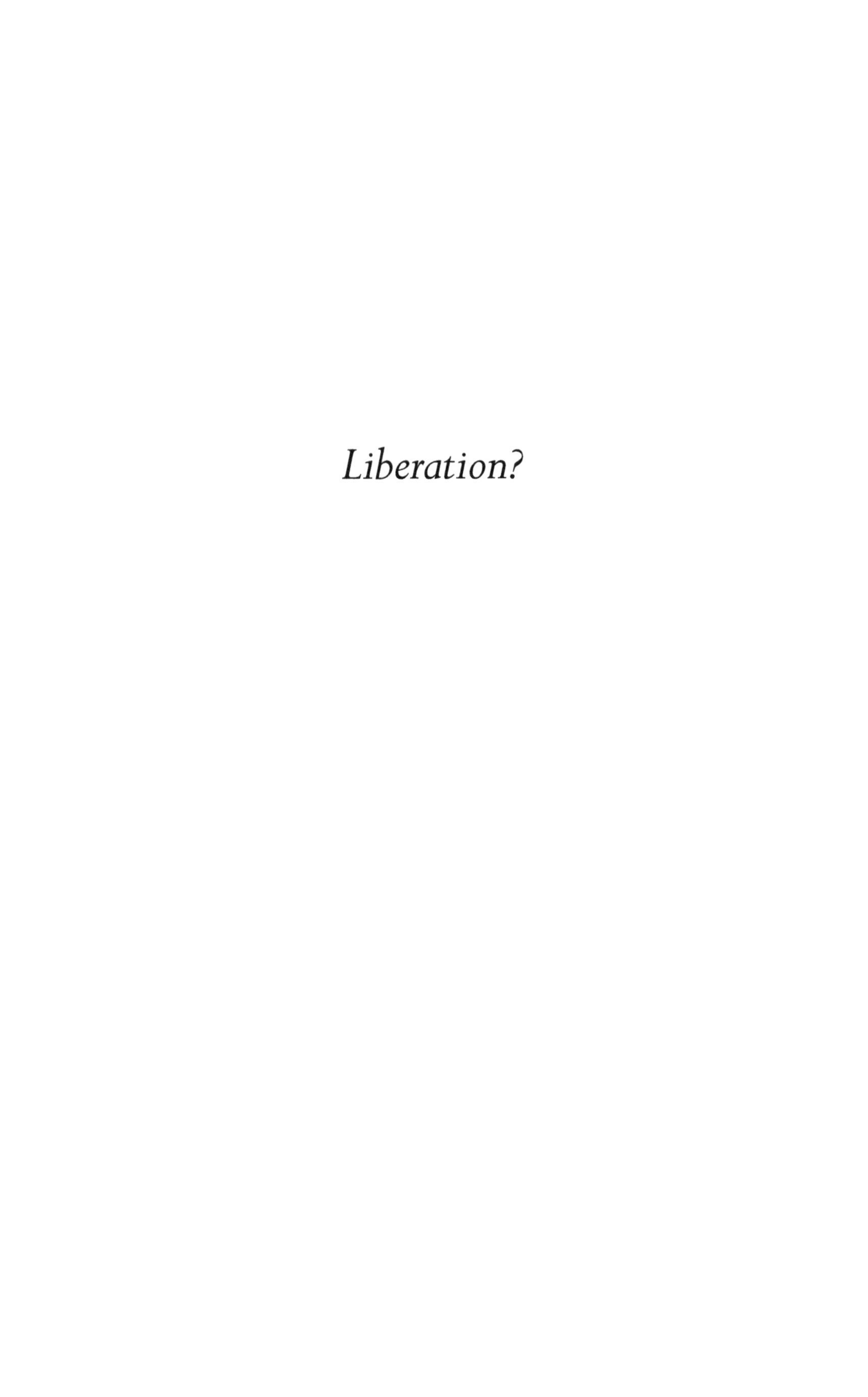

Liberation?

114

Who are they?

Our district turned into a battleground. Tanks and cannons joined the bombers to keep us in the cellar praying for silence and life. We stopped talking. We were waiting. Vica and I continued gathering the remnants of candles, but her mother had no more matches and we had to borrow her father's lighter to melt the wax. Mr Bauer soon ran out of patience and told us to sit still and stop wasting the lighter fluid on our games. No more candle making.

I went back to sit between Anyu and Grandma and put a pillow over my head because the plaster was falling after each detonation. Anyu hugged me and whispered into my hair, "I hope Apu's all right."

I leaned on her and fell asleep in her lap, only waking when Mr Kelemen entered the shelter in the early morning. Anyu's watch showed a phosphorescent five o'clock. Many of the others were still asleep. Beside the last lonely candle flickering by the makeshift lavatory entrance, there was no light, no way of telling that the night was over. Our shelter was like a tomb.

That was the day when everything changed.

*

Old Kelemen shuffled to his armchair and coughed before he spoke. Then he said it as loud as he could manage, "They are here." He said it twice.

I sat up and saw Mr Bauer get up, take off his armband and put his truncheon under the mattress of his wife, Vica's mother. Everybody was suddenly awake, shuffling things, straightening jackets and scarves, folding blankets.

Nobody asked, "Who are they?"

A wave of muted grumbling mingled with sibilant whispers. Mrs Kelemen pulled off her wedding ring and stuffed it into her bra stretching her pullover over it.

Vica's mother rubbed her fingers against the wick of a cold candle and started to smear the soot on Vica's face.

Grandma did the same. I tried to pull my head away from her fingers, but she grabbed the back of my head and whispered: "Sit still. You must look old." She pulled off her kerchief, letting her white hair fall over her face, and tied it on my head pulling it down to shade my face. "You must look old like me," she said. "They look for the young."

I didn't ask her why.

The radio had told us so many times, we all knew. "To peel potatoes," they called it. But they said it was worse.

It had to be much worse. Even Anyu smeared soot under her eyes, and Mrs Kelemen, who looked old anyway, was doing the same. The few men seemed restless and stared at the floor as if they were ashamed of something.

Then we sat frozen. Rigid. Silence spread, the silence of apprehension.

It was a long wait until a noisy clumping on the steps broke through the chill followed by loud words we couldn't understand. I leaned on Grandma, who pulled me closer. Anyu sat bundled in a black shawl, motionless behind us. I lowered my head and hunched my shoulders to look old.

Four soldiers appeared in the door. They held their guns pointing at us, ready to shoot. They were dusty and muddy and they had darting eyes. Two of them looked Chinese, with high cheekbones, short and stocky. Their hats had fur flaps dangling over their ears, and they were alert and moved fast, scanning our faces and talking briskly.

They poked at Vica's grandfather who stood up and they looked under his chair, lifted a mattress or two, but moved too fast to search carefully. Their uniforms were loose and warm with thick quilted jackets, much warmer looking than the German uniforms, which were tidier and tighter with clean, shiny boots, more like they looked in the war movies.

Then they disappeared.

Everyone started talking at once. We rearranged our waiting, knowing that there was more to come.

Next, an even faster stamping noise on the stairs made us fall silent again. Two taller soldiers came through the shelter door in neater uniforms and with stuff sewn on their sleeves. They were obviously officers. The taller of them asked in German if anybody spoke German. One of the new neighbours who took over the Kendes' place answered him. He slowly stood up leaning on his stick with one hand and holding a dark blanket wrapped around his shoulders with the other. He was old and shaky. I only knew him slightly because he was too new in the house to matter. His wife looked as old as he. I think their name was Bolla. Or Barna. His German was not as good as Apu's; he stumbled a lot as he translated the officer's words very slowly.

"He says we can't keep guns. If we have one, we should hand it over. Right now. He asks, anyone has a weapon?"

Heads shook. "Nem!"

Somebody said, "Nyet." Then we all cottoned on and said "nyet." And "nein", but not very loud, more in a mumbling way.

"He says that we are not to hide soldiers either."

"Nyet. Nein. Nem."

"He says he's a captain. He says we are free now. He says they came to free us from German oppression. And from the rule of the Hungarian lackeys of the Germans. He says that if we have a problem or complaint, we can go and report it to the local headquarters of the Soviet Army. He says, he wishes us well."

The taller officer stopped talking. He rearranged the glasses on his nose and patted old Bolla on the shoulder, who swayed under the weight of his hand. The other, shorter officer, who was pale and skinny, didn't seem interested in anything his comrade had said, but kept a sharp eye on all of us and his hand on his gun as he started towards the exit.

They both left in a hurry.

Somebody piped up asking Bolla, "Where is their headquarters?"

"How should I know?" said the old man as he sat down beside his wife.

115

Potato peeling

For a while there was what seemed like a procession of soldiers. We sat stiffly, like stone statues on our chairs and mattresses, afraid to make a move. Vica's father left the shelter door open, and we could hear sporadic gunfire and tanks hurtling by. The sirens were silent.

Next four Russians arrived, all of them short and squat in their quilted *pufajkas*, with guns slung over their shoulders, hand grenades stuck in their belts. They held up a wristwatch and motioned us to show ours. When nobody moved, they poked Mr Kelemen, who stood up and lifted his arms over his head signaling surrender. They pulled up his sleeves and saw that he had no watches on either of his wrists and pushed him to sit down. Then Mrs Kelemen handed over her watch and a few of the new tenants in the old Jewish apartments, whose names I didn't know yet, also volunteered to hand over theirs. The soldiers gathered the loot, arguing about a few bits that looked like gold, and left.

The next three soldiers were taller and staggering drunk. They came looking for women to peel potatoes. Nobody volunteered. They looked us over, but were too inebriated to see much with their unsteady torches. When it was Grandma's turn to be spotlighted, she lifted her face and opened her toothless mouth wide, stuck out her tongue and shook her head in contempt.

They burst out laughing, and one of them shouted something like *starya babushka.* Then they made some awkward moves, which Anyu explained later were obscene, and climbed up the steps holding onto each other.

After that we decided that it was not safer below than upstairs. Anyu talked with Vica's mother and offered our airshaft as a safe place to hide for her and Vica. Everybody scattered, and we all moved in a hurry carrying our bedding with us. When we entered our apartment, Apu was there greeting us with a hug. He didn't have to hide any more.

Mrs Bauer turned to me, "And you told Vica that he was somewhere in Russia."

I said nothing. How could I tell her that we were afraid of her husband?

"Let's practice," said Anyu and she led her and Vica to the bathroom window.

116

How to behave encountering enemy soldiers

You must keep all doors open because facing a locked door they sense resistance and may blast it open and enter with rifles ready to shoot they don't speak your language you can't depend on words only the mask you wear for their searching eyes don't hide your eyes because they will suspect malice, hostile thoughts and deadly plans but present an open face unless you are a young in which case it is wise to smear some soot around your lips and eyes no need to smile that can be read as sarcasm they get itchy fingers if faced with contempt or signs of superiority they expect gratitude serious demeanor a tinge of dignity without false humility or greasy servility which may make them suspect that you have something to hide don't wrap yourself in blankets which may conceal weapons it pays to learn a word or two just in case but never argue or contradict saying a soothing "good, good" comes in handy even if in the context "good, good" makes no sense it sounds reassuring for nervous soldiers trigger-happy and lost in a foreign land just say it firmly and slowly never in a hurrying manner if he is German it should be "sehr gut" if Russian "harasho" learn "OK and "swell" say "tres bon" or "foarte bine" with concurrent nodding of the head

don't try to use "yes" and "no" because those words can be much more tricky you don't know what they are asking and if you say yes to their hurried question "are you hiding some grenades or guns or are you a soldier who just changed from uniform into pyjamas" your "yes" may turn you into an instant enemy combatant or you may say no to a question which you judge hostile due to the tone of voice and in panic you protest “no, no” “nyet, nyet” or “nein, nein” but the question may be “are you ready to provide billet to a dozen tired troopers for the night” or “are you glad to be liberated” in either case a vehement “no, no” may compel them to take you away to an undisclosed destination for an unspecified time or for forever.

117

Looting coal from the factory

It is good to look out the window again. The blackout panels are off, stacked in the corner behind Grandma's sewing machine. They appear dusty and useless, the paper starting to peel off in the corners, even the blackened outsides have faded into their original “wrapping paper brown”.

It seems that everything has changed, everything is shabbier, worn out. Only the freshly fallen snow on the rooftops stays as white and clean as ever, and there is a new kind of buzz in the yard full of *Ruszkis*. Their strange talk mingles with the smell of boiling soup in the huge container on the top of their busily smoking “field kitchen” under our window. Good warm soup. Some unspecified pieces of meat, mostly gristle, float around under chunky cabbage leaves.

Yesterday, when the cook gave me a bowlful, Grandma didn't let on that she approved, only growled that she hated to see me begging. She was busy disapproving a lot of things that happened and freely articulated her frequent displeasure aroused by various people, especially by politicians who made wars, by bankers and bureaucrats, sometimes even by God Almighty who didn't stop them. Her words were accompanied by the banging of pots and pans on the stove with extra force.

That morning she was angry with the weather when she was trying to open a window stuck with ice.

It was so cold, that the *Ruszkis* wrapped in their thick *pufajkas* were slapping their thighs as they were standing around the fire waiting for soup. They seemed to be dancing while they blew breath-clouds into their fists and tapped their boots on the ground.

Our place was warm. Anyu kept stoking the fire in the potbelly, feeding it with the coal we stole from the factory yard.

Buckets and buckets of black coal, but it was all right, it was war, as they said, and we could freeze without them.

Besides, everyone else was doing it. Even the Kelemens, the Bauers as well as strangers from the houses around us swarmed in armed with buckets and sacks. They set to shovelling, heaving, slithering over the heaps of briquettes. My face and hands were covered with coal dust by the time we lugged our buckets home.

It was scary to watch the rats, black and shiny, escaping the sudden noise in the shed, jumping over the shovels, running in all directions. Big fat rats.

"They got fat feeding on the dead," Grandma said.

118

Apu looks for Ómama

Anyu sounds worried when Apu wraps his scarf around his neck and puts on a wool cap getting ready to search for his mother.

His old winter coat looks too elegant, Anyu says.

Luckily, it is worn at the cuffs and shiny at the elbows, so Anyu consents that it may work today because it is still snowing, and it will soon be covered enough with snowflakes to pass without notice.

She is fussing: be careful, stop if they shout, never, never run, don't start talking German unless you are stopped by an intelligent officer who listens to you before he shoots. If it is only an illiterate infantryman, he may shoot before he listens, thinking that you are a German soldier trying to pass as a civilian, and you would be…

"Stop it," says Apu, "Do you think I am an idiot? Don't worry."

But it is no use. Anyu always worries. That is the main difference between them: Apu pretending not to care about most things, and Anyu looking worried with her eyebrows rising and almost meeting in a sharp peak above her nose. She has a way of foreseeing the worst.

I sit shivering on the edge of the bed and watch them carry on.

"They are still shooting," says Anyu.

"Only in Buda," Apu says.

"But the shells land here in Pest."

"I'll dodge them." He gives her a hug.

His hugs are never quick squeezes. They are long embraces that make Anyu rise on her tiptoes, and they always end with a light smack on her bottom. A signal to move apart.

"Where will you start?"

"I'll go through every house in the ghetto."

"Every house still standing," Anyu sighs and turns away.

I stand up still shivering when the door closes behind Apu.

119

Waiting for Ómama

I have mulled over every detail of that day for years and still do.

Tension permeated every word said or left unsaid. The sound of cannons booming, the SS and Wehmacht still shelling us from Buda Castle, was a staccato of menace. Hitler ordered his soldiers to fight for their Vaterland, no matter what.

Our fears hardly lifted with the arrival of a new language, Russian sounds I never heard before, a language that was supposed to be barbaric (we were told at school), but which (as I later learned) happened to be the language of Tolstoy and Pushkin, Chernyshevsky and Gogol.

"When you read *War and Peace* all the way through, you'll be an adult," Apu said years ago.

"Is it that difficult?"

"It is that long,"

"When did you read it?"

"I haven't finished it yet," he said.

Russia always appeared in movies as a wild place. It meant winter and war. Muzhiks in muddy rags, Cossacks galloping on wild horses and tzarinas dressed in diamond-studded gowns presiding over tables laden with caviar. It was another kind of Russia that burst into 4/B Lehel Street.

Like most children surrounded by a mother tongue alone, I couldn't imagine another language constantly filling the air and being as effective as my own. God had created the world in Hungarian because God himself spoke Hungarian.

Now that the siege was almost over and Soviet soldiers were bivouacked in the yard, I listened to snatches of conversation laced with laughter and what sounded like angry arguments rising from below. I was determined to make sense of it and took up my place by the window, breathed on the glass and rubbed it with my fingers to melt the frost in a neat porthole-circle trying to keep an eye on what was going on.

A few officers came through the gate and talked to the cook.

I was hungry, my permanent state then, and I wished they would leave the cook alone. It was easy to tell that they were officers. They looked neater and acted bossier than the cook. Maybe they were ordering him not to give away any of their precious soup to Hungarian children. He turned his back, gesticulated, shook his head and kept shaking it long after they left.

Across the yard, Paula stepped outside and swept away the snow from the door with her broom, doing her daily ritual of cleaning regardless of the changing fortunes of war. That's the way I remember her. Paula, the rag-shaker, the broom-wielder. She was always the same: a small, rotund figure wearing an apron, stepping out of the Baum's kitchen that was bigger than our whole apartment, leaning over the rail, shaking and folding before she dived back into her realm. I was glad to see her that day, because she sulked and acted like a hermit in the air raid shelter after they took away the Baums and she had to share the apartment with strangers.

She only started talking when a stray German shell fired from Buda hit the wall of her room. A large hole appeared and she was busy boarding it up with a piece of plywood, ignoring the Russian soldiers. Grandma said that Mr Kelemen helped her nail it up, but I didn't see him.

I concentrated on watching her through her kitchen window after she went inside. She was bending and reaching, adjusting the kerchief she wore on her head. While I was waiting for Apu to bring Ómama, I forced myself to focus on Paula who was not a relative, nor a close friend. Waiting was easier if I tried not to think.

The day dimmed. It was getting late.

120

Ómama's many homes

In the evenings the streets were more dangerous, and there was no sign of Apu. Did he get shot? Grabbed and taken away? Will he escape again?

I sat down in his chair by the table, then moved it closer to the fire and tried to continue thinking of something else. Something in the past that seemed already set, more predictable than the present.

Food.

The good food we couldn't have, we had to go without, was the best to think about. First, I recalled the croissants Ómama used to soak in boiling milk and sprinkle with poppy seed and sugar. They melted in my mouth. How she smiled every time she handed me a full plate! And how she asked if I wanted more. I always did.

Anyu interrupted my daydream when she put on a coat and went somewhere without telling me where, while Grandma heated water over the potbelly stove that turned red on its side and warmed my back.

When Anyu came back, she announced that if Apu found Ómama, there would be room for her to stay in the maid's room next door, where she could have privacy and comfort.

"It has a good bed and nobody's using it at the moment. It's full of the Kendes' leftover stuff, but the new people promised to clear out the room soon," she said turning towards me. "Until then, you will sleep with us in our bed and Ómama will sleep on your *sezlony.*"

True, there was hardly enough room even for the three of us in our apartment. Now, with Grandma, we were already four. She slept on a collapsible cot in the kitchen taking up all the space there with her feet having to fit under the table.

Ómama had never lived with us. I only saw her in her own flat, first in a big house by the railroad tracks, close to the Nyugati Railroad Station, high up on the third floor. She had a balcony facing Lehel Street where she kept her pots of geraniums neatly lined up by the rail. Apu photographed her there with me standing next to her.

Then she moved to a smaller room on the ground floor in Ipoly Street, only a few blocks from us. We could enter her room directly from the street, just up a few stone steps. It must have been a shop before it became her home, and it had no kitchen, but she could cook on a tiny gas stove. It was always warm in there and smelled good. I spent many days with her, watching her sew new dresses and aprons for me.

She proudly told me that at one point in her life, when she had a big enough kitchen with a bigger table she used for cutting up cloth, she had an apron business, "Aprons for butchers, big white ones for bakers and fancy, frilly ones for waitresses. Lots of aprons. Your father, still a boy, helped with delivery."

Now Apu had to look for her.

When he said "ghetto", he made it sound like hell.

We were all waiting: Grandma, nervously noisy in the kitchen, Anyu scrubbing the tub in the bathroom without saying a word.

Were they also thinking about Ómama?

Yes, I used to love to survey Ipoly Street from Ómama's narrow window before the war. Across the way was the shop of a welder, whose torch threw a blinding light through his open door. The mask he wore, the huge gloves, the noise of metalwork livened up the street.

The last place I visited her was different. Only once did I see the room where she was ordered to move. It was on the third floor of a big house on *Szent István Körút,* in a house designated for Jews. She was crammed into a tiny space, more like a hole in the wall, opening from a hallway. In another, bigger room several other people were packed together.

Ómama, after asking somebody I didn't know for permission to enter, took me into that crowded room to show me a grand piano. She introduced me to a very old woman, who had blue veins bulging on the back of her hands when she lifted the lid of the piano and played for me, while I sat on a chair and admired the shiny ivory and ebony keys under her fingers. Then she suddenly slammed down the lid and turned towards me.

"Awful," she said. "It badly needs tuning. He would be aghast if he heard me."

Back in Ómama's windowless cubbyhole that was hardly big

enough to turn around, I asked her who was the person who would be aghast about that great piano.

"Franz Liszt," she said. "She was Liszt's pupil long ago, when she was young."

I was hoping to hear her play again on her out-of-tune piano in that room jammed with dark furniture, suitcases, and cushions, but soon the siege started, and I never paid another visit.

Now Ómama will be living with us. Maybe she will serve my favourite scalded croissants with tons of poppy seed again.

I knew well that at the moment there was no fresh *kifli* to be had, not in Budapest. And we had no poppy seed and not a single spoonful of sugar left. Our larder was practically empty except for the depleted sack of dry peas Grandma boiled in water and fried in the lard she scraped from the bottom of the blue tub I'd carried on my back from Püski.

It would be a miracle if Ómama arrived with a big bag of powdered sugar.

121

Ómama's derelict suitcase

It was pitch dark by the time Apu knocked on the door, so I did not see him come up the stairs. With him was Ómama and a suitcase. But she was not the same Ómama.

She was bent and covered with a dirty blanket, shivering and silent, held up by Apu, who eased her down on his armchair slowly, as if she were breakable. Everybody was silent for a moment.

Then the blanket slithered off Ómama's head and I noticed a smell, a smell I've never smelled before. A mixture of cellar dampness and candlewick smoke, old cheese and kerosene fumes filled the room.

Anyu brought towels from the bathroom. Grandma slowly undressed Ómama, who was shrunken and tottery enough that two of them had to help her to the bathroom where Apu was filling the tub. He left as soon as Ómama was lowered into the water.

That is when I noticed that most of Grandma's previously noisy bustle had to do with the pots of extra water she had heated in preparation for this bath. Our *autogeiser* could never generate enough hot water. She bundled up the clothes she had taken off Ómama and threw them one by one into the fire while cursing the lice even I could see crawling around as I was huddling close to the stove. The fire roared and the flames leapt high as they caught cotton and wool. Grandma slammed the lid closed and raised Ómama's skirt, towards the light. "Still has some wear in it," she mumbled. "Worth saving."

She stashed it into our tin bucket filled with water and bleach, and I watched her wash it the next day under the kitchen sink and iron it with the hottest imaginable iron, after it dried enough to turn from soggy to damp. She ironed slowly as she carefully raised with her nails the stitches around the waistband showing me the hiding dead lice as she scraped them out and slammed the iron over them.

It is strange that I found it entirely natural that after all those years, when I never heard Grandma even mention Ómama's name, on that day they acted as intimates. She allowed Grandma to undress her. To soap her back. To wash her hair. And she did this so vigorously, I thought Ómama would cry out. She soaped and washed, and soaped and washed again, and ladled warm water over her head. Then she took a comb and started to comb her wet hair and soap it again and rubbed her head with such passion that poor Ómama was buckling all over the place. Anyu had to hold her by both shoulders to stop her falling backwards.

I stood behind the bathroom door and stared. Nobody told me to go away.

I heard Anyu say, "Something light."

"Fried peas are ready," Grandma said.

"Can't be fried peas. We still have a bit of flour, don't we? I'll make a quick *köménymag* (caraway seed) soup. They starved her. The bastards."

They lifted Ómama out of the tub and wrapped her in towels.

"Move out of the way," Grandma ordered me finally.

They made Ómama lie down on my bed and that's when she looked at me and tried to smile.

"Talk to her," Grandma said and motioned me to sit on the edge of the *sezlony*.

"Ómama. Are you warm enough?"

"I am. Yes, I am," she said. I leaned forward to hear her. She moved her hand from under the towel and held my hand while she drifted off to sleep. Then Anyu came with the *köménymag* soup and propped up her head on pillows and made her swallow.

I didn't ask Ómama about poppy seed. I was thinking about the clothes that burned in the potbelly. Grandma had never put any clothes in the fire before. On the contrary, she mended and patched everything.

I hated this war that turned everything upside down and made people do what they never did before. I hated those who made Ómama into a skeleton and covered her with dirt and lice and bad smells.

I watched her as she drifted into a deep sleep, until Anyu sent me to brush my teeth and told me to lie down. "You'll be with us tonight," she said again. "Don't disturb Ómama."

I crawled into the double bed and turned towards the wall pretending to sleep, but I heard Apu and Anyu whispering over my head.

“I searched for her all over, went through a dozen houses, asked everyone I could,” Apu said. “Bodies were stacked up by the gate like firewood. Stiff. Frozen. I found her sitting on a chair in a cellar. She was alone with the dead. Those who could walk, had already left. She recognized me. Hardly could get up. Hardly could walk.”

“Did you give her the bread?”

So that’s where the piece of black bread the *Ruszki* cook gave me yesterday went. I was looking for it, wanting a bite. Anyu gave it to him for Ómama. Now we have her to feed too. For a moment I was ashamed of my thoughts.

“When they were ordered into the ghetto, they herded them on the street. They put their bundles on a truck and made them walk behind. She said that when they got there, she couldn’t find her basket that had jars of jam, some lard and a bag of flour in it. Even some sugar. Somebody handed her this beat up suitcase instead, full of useless junk.”

“What’s in it?”

“We’ll look tomorrow.”

I fell asleep thinking of the suitcase.

What if it were full of powdered sugar?

122

My first watch and dried peas

Ómama, sitting up in bed, supervised the opening of her suitcase. Apu snapped the lid open, and a miscellany of women’s cosmetics appeared alongside a lacey nightgown and a negligee, several bead necklaces and a small pocket watch. Ómama lifted out the watch and held it to her ear.

"You'll have to wind it up," she said turning to me as she handed it over. "It is yours. The rest is of no use."

"What should we do with it?" asked Apu.

"I don't care. It reminds me…" Ómama didn't finish. She turned to the wall. "Let me sleep, please."

The watch was dirty, and some fuzz under the lid stopped the minute hand from moving.

I can remember every detail of my first watch, recall the pinkish porcelain encircling its rim and the iridescent blue enamel of its back lid. I admired the gold second hand which I could move around with my finger and which in turn could move the hour and minute hands that were thicker and wider, but slower to move.

I held it tightly in my fist and went to the window. The Russians were buzzing below. I will not let them have it. I must find for it a safe hiding place.

123

Weevils and accordions

The factory yard was swarming with soldiers. The bowlegged cook was stirring his giant cauldron of soup. A hulking flat-faced mechanic was leaning into the engine of a mud-spattered truck while another soldier kept trying to start the engine that heaved and died, heaved and died with gradually diminishing gusto. Officers came and went. A gaunt soldier in a faded green *pufajka* was chopping cabbage, and Grandma kept telling me to stay away from the window.

But I enjoyed the spectacle of military life behind battle lines, the casual way these men spent their time cooking, jostling each other, mending their gear.

Once, when a new group arrived it included an older soldier, a small man with a big smile and missing front teeth. I watched him as he sat down at the back of a truck parked under the Kelemens' window and started playing a melancholy number on a small accordion. I later learned that it was the famous song of Volga boatmen pulling ropes in unison, more a lament than just a work song. His baritone and the voices of the others joining in and singing along with him filled the courtyard with sorrow.

The most often played song with a bold, joyous melody was *Polyushka Polye*, which later we learned to sing in Russian class in the *gimnázium*.

"Stop showing yourself in the window," Grandma snapped again. She was sitting by the table picking weevils out of the dry peas she arranged into a diminishing unpicked pile and a growing pile that had passed inspection. "Come and help me if you want to eat tomorrow."

I hated the dry peas we had to swallow every night as fried patties or cooked in a soup. We never could find all the weevils. They floated up to the top of the boiling water like black dots of dirt.

"They won't kill you," Grandma said when she noticed disgust on my face. "Think of them as meat."

Time and time again

You say today is more alive than yesterday,
and last week is closer than 1944.
A fly that landed on the milk jug way back then
is less pertinent than an ant of this moment.

Is last week much closer than 1944?
You say I must stop wallowing in memories
and stay with the ant of the moment on my plate.
But how? The century, a tired whore, a tease,

offers the lull of a wallow in memories.
I am looking at a pure azure summer sky.
I am a child of a spent century, the whore.
Jewel-like silver planes glitter high as they fly.

I stand dazzled by the pure azure summer sky.
Fighters dart among the droning Constellations
jewel-like silver planes glittering as they fly.
They thunder over us to bomb railroad stations.

Darting fighters herd the droning Constellations.
I bite into a ripe pear fallen on the grass
as they pass above me to bomb railroad stations.
An open-beaked rooster gives a shrill warning cry.

I bite into the ripe pear picked up from the grass
savouring the sweetness and the resonant earth.
The startled rooster tilts one eye towards the sky,
and geese in a tight gaggle tread the dust nearby.

Seduced by the sweetness and the resonant sky,
I count the planes heavy with bombs and guns,
as geese hiss and gaggle with trembling tongues nearby,
I wish for one to crash and to see the pilot fall.

Counting hundreds of planes heavy with bombs and guns
I see some trailing smoke and streaks of flaming runs.
Mesmerized as they dive, I watch the pilots tumble
White petals of parachutes float in the pure azure.

I see the trailing smoke and flames smear the sky.
I am a child then, gulping air as I am today,
and still see those petals as they fly,
and still taste the sweet juice of pears.

I am that child gripped by the same intensity
filled with the same open-eyed wonder today,
the child sticky with the juice of countless summers
standing scarred by battles that go on to this day.

Those who say that today has buried yesterday,
and last week is closer than 1944
do not comprehend the child trembling, overwhelmed
by the unravelled, droll jig of the floating dead.

124

The billets

Ómama slept a lot, and soon we settled into a considerate routine of silence for her sake.

"She needs it," said Anyu.

Even Apu attempted to tiptoe around her.

We would talk behind closed doors in the kitchen, where Grandma retained her hegemony. She walked around with her hands crossed over her belly. Her apron was wrinkled. Nobody ironed anything for weeks and weeks. Everything was a mess.

An unexploded bomb was still lying where the Hungarian soldiers who disabled it last month left it under the second sandbagged window of the shelter.

Whenever the Russian cook in the courtyard refilled my bowl with his boiling borscht, all of us would share a few spoonfuls. Even Grandma condescended to have some because our goose fat bin in the pantry only had some scrapings left at the bottom, and we were hungry for bits of meat.

There was no way to search for food in the city while the battle over Buda was raging. The boom of shelling kept the streets empty of traffic with the exception of Russian tanks and trucks rattling by. Occasional gunfire erupted startlingly close, but nobody knew who was shooting whom. German, Russian, Hungarian guns, to us all sounded the same.

Grandma slept in the kitchen between the table and the gas stove, Ómama on my *sezlony* and Apu and Anyu on their bed with me on the edge by the wall. There was not much to do other than wait, so we went to bed early to keep warm. Then one evening we woke to a commotion in the courtyard. Engines rattled, brakes wheezed and doors slammed accompanied by shouts that made us sit up in alarm.

Soon, someone banged on our door and a tall Russian soldier stood there yakking at Grandma who blocked his way shivering in her flannel nightgown. I was sure that he was an officer because he seemed to have authority over the other two soldiers standing behind him gun in hand.

Without a word, Ómama slowly got up, wrapped a blanket over her shoulders and limped to the door.

The Russian was getting impatient with Grandma by the time Ómama appeared, and his voice was louder and more demanding.

'Shto dyelaty?' interrupted Ómama. Her voice was loud and clear for the first time since Apu brought her home, quite a change.

The soldier turned to her and slowed down a bit, seeing that he faced two *babushkas* standing in his way, relieved that at least one of was able to speak.

He took off his fur hat with the big flaps protecting his ears, stepped closer to Ómama and bent down to her level like a man in the movies about to ask a girl to dance. Ómama nodded and answered him, making a move with her hand, a gesture that took in the whole room crowded with beds.

Then she turned to Apu and said, "Ilya here says that they are looking for places to sleep."

Apu said, "Tell him that we would be glad to oblige, but this is a one room flat, and five of us take up all the room."

Ómama gestured with both arms. This time the blanket slipped off her shoulders and I could see underneath it Grandma's wool scarf and Apu's flannel pajamas.

The officer who had a big red nose, probably frozen in Siberia, kept walking around the place while Ómama kept talking to him. He looked into the WC for the second time and shook his head. Maybe he didn't like what he saw. And no wonder. How could we have everything spic-and-span when the Germans were still shooting down on us from Buda, and the place still shook now and then.

Ómama said: "Ilya says that he has to place his men in this house. Ilya says this is war. He'd rather sleep at home in his own bed in Omsk."

He put back his hat, and on his way out said something to the two soldiers standing by the door. They came in and searched the place rummaging through every drawer and messing up the bookshelf as they peered behind the books.

"Looking for guns and ammunition," Ómama said.

When they left slamming the door behind them, we all got up, tidied the place and put on coats and headscarves. Anyu bundled me back under the covers and took up a position behind Apu, who sat on the edge of the bed.

Next we had four new soldiers by the door.

They brought in their packs and put them down on the floor under the window. Apu, trying to look agreeable, gestured towards the chairs, but they ignored him as they sat down. Two of them looked much older than Apu, and one of them must have been no more than 16 or 17. The fourth soldier came in last, and he sat down last by the table resting his head over his arms. He fell asleep immediately with his face buried in in the sleeves of his dirty *pufajka.*

The taller middle-aged one, whose pockmarked face I can never forget, said something and looked around. Silence followed. Then he coughed and said something again.

This time Ómama stirred and answered him. He turned to her and kept talking while she responded by nodding her head.

Apu interrupted, 'What does he say?"

Ómama lifted a hand towards the mouth of the soldier and started translating. 'He says that they are very tired. They need to sleep. He says that they had no sleep for days. They have to eat first. He says they have bread and some bacon. Wants hot water for tea.'

Grandma stood up and went into the kitchen.

The young one followed her to see what she was doing, then went out the front door leaving it open long enough for a chill blast to come through.

The pockmarked yelled after him.

'He says to close the door," Ómama translated automatically.

When the young one came back, they started unpacking their bundles, taking off their hats and unbuttoning their jackets. The shorter soldier who looked Chinese nudged the sleeping one, but all he got out of him were a few angry grunts.

At that the pockmarked soldier shouted 'Ogony!'

Ómama cried, "Fire!'

The sleeper jumped up grabbing a revolver from his belt, causing his mates to burst out laughing. He shook his head and sat down again opening his bag and lifting out a loaf of dark bread.

We had already tasted Russian bread by then, courtesy of the soup kitchen. It was hard and bitter, meant to last.

We sat and watched them spread their bounty on our table. Out came a slab of bacon that looked smoked and still had salt crystals stuck on its tough skin, probably commandeered from somebody's larder in a village, another loaf of bread, a bulging linen bag tied with a string that turned out to hold precious lumps of sugar and a green bottle half full with some drink. The young soldier uncorked it and took a swig, but the short one grabbed it out of his hand and put the cork back telling him something in anger.

Ómama translated, 'You fool! Don't guzzle the vodka. It's for all of us.'

They sliced the bacon, scraping every last bit off the skin.

The skinny, older soldier, who turned out to be bald when he took off his fur hat, wiped his knife on his sleeve and sliced the bread slowly, with care, perhaps aware that all eyes in the room were glued to the slices as they fell from the blade.

When he put down the knife, he turned to Ómama and said something. She translated, 'He is asking whether we wished to join them for a bite.'

Soon we were chewing the smoked bacon and the hard bread, sipping the tea from mugs Grandma brought in from the kitchen. Best of all there was sugar in the tea, lumps of white sugar, a taste of luxury we had gone without for a while.

Ómama had to go on talking in both languages, visibly proud of her new role as an interpreter, reminding us that she knew Szlovák, She had never met a Russian before, but her Szlovák seemed to work all right.

As the steam of the tea and the smell of the vodka generously dribbled into each mug filled the small room overpowering the smell of bacon, the smoke of the rough Russian cigarettes and the odours of war, we all seemed to unwind.

The pockmarked soldier whose nose noticeably reddened by the heat, took out a wrinkled leather wallet from his breast pocket and pulled out a photo. Ómama handed it around saying 'This is Oleg's wife and their three children.'

We saw a slender woman standing in front of a tractor, holding a baby in her arms. On her left stood a boy, maybe three, sucking his thumb, and on her right, an older girl half hidden behind her mother's skirt.

Out came more photos from pockets and tobacco tins. The bald soldier showed a wife and a son standing next to a tree and the tattered portrait of an old woman whose face was shaded by a dark kerchief. She was sitting on a stool next to a rooster.

"His grandmother," Ómama said. "He says I look like her."

The young soldier who had two wristwatches visible on each arm, handed around the portrait of a pretty girl in overalls standing by a machine on a factory floor and holding in her hands a piece of paper unfurled against her breast.

"She is Tamara, showing the award she received for her work," Ómama said slowly, trying to overcome her growing fatigue.

Father ordered me to lie down and turn to the wall. Grandma was gathering up the plates. The soldiers started to yawn and stretch. They unrolled their blankets and lay down on the floor between the *sezlony* and our bed, tucking their jackets under their head. Anyu snuggled up to me. Apu put himself between her and the soldiers.

It took some time for me to fall asleep. Maybe it was the dash of vodka in my tea. Soon all I could hear was heavy breathing mingled with snores. Then I heard the young soldier get up and stagger out to the corridor leaving the door open again. A cold blast of air hit my face, and I could hear him piss over the rail into the courtyard.

125

Survival rush

When the guns fells silent in Budapest in 1945, people emerged from their underground holes slowly at first, then in a rush.

A rush to find food, firewood, medicine, to find relatives, to clear the rubble, to start bartering, a rush to find out who had died, where and how. And a rush to talk, to recount near misses, to tell their survival stories.

Coming home

from Stalingrad
from the Don
from Poland
from Dachau
from Serbia
from Berlin
from Rome
the year of 1945
was the year of coming home

from battlefields and death camps
from copper mines
muddy trenches
bomb craters and air raid shelters
crossing ice-clad rivers
charred forests
snow-clad hills and
churned up plains
coming home on foot
on crowded trains
begging rides on trucks
ox-carts
dragging sleds or
pushing barrows
starved
debilitated
the call of home never faded
it grew louder
reverberated

battered soldiers
lame amputees
orphaned children
dazed refugees
took to the road
fed by the hope
of a warm hearth
a table set
with forks and knives
a hot tub
a chunk of soap
fresh sheets
on a soft bed
a home
to be had

126

Roads of death

My father changed from a hiding man into a feverishly active writer He penned a book entitled "The Novel of the Bor Death Road" in a hurry, trying to gather up his still acute memories, events and voices only a few months distant, in the form of a narrative. He wanted to get it on the street fast, into people's hands, making them know what went on in labour camps and on the roads. It was published under the aegis of Gábor Áron Publishers.

I recall my mother typing the stacks of manuscript bent over the dining table and my father walking up and down, dictating inserts whenever another incident came to his mind that needed to be included.

When it was printed and ready for sale, we stacked Apu's book, alongside other new books published by the victims and other volumes about the politics of war, on a rickety table he had found somewhere. We stood the table in the front of a burnt out empty shop on Szent István Körút among other tables where people were selling used clothing, antiques and family heirlooms, anything to make a *pengő*. I remember how the hawkers jostled for the prime spots closer to the sidewalk where people lingered, pleased to be able to shop and browse again.

At times I was left in charge of the table and had to learn to answer questions. So I had to read Apu's book and memorize the harrowing details, some of which I had heard him tell my mother before.

The word "novel" in the title is unfortunately accurate.

This book, without footnotes, named some of the victims and perpetrators and recorded true details of the events he had witnessed along the way, but because it was written in the style of his earlier, pre-war books, and because he spiced the story with witty dialogue and romance, it fell short of being a meticulous modern documentary.

In spite of his narrative tone however, as an observant survivor, he depicted the dark days of the labour camp and the slaughter along the way from Bor to Baja in evocative vignettes that only a watchful eyewitness could record.

127

In the maid's room

Everything speeded up before my eyes. The Kendes survived with the exception of a daughter-in-law who was gassed. They moved back from the ghetto. The couple that took over their place was relegated to one room and Mrs Kende, smaller and thinner than she was before the war, reclaimed two rooms for her son Sam and for herself. The kitchen was divided into two halves with a chalk line on the floor, and the hall and the bathroom were shared, leading to endless disputations.

Ómama moved into the maid's room as arranged. Her condition worsened, and we were in and out all the time looking after her. The doctor talked about blood pressure, heart irregularities, exhaustion, depression, anaemia and some other unpronounceable ailments. Her biggest pain was in her legs that swelled up, mostly in her left foot that turned red and inflamed. She was bedridden.

Grandma and Anyu washed her with a sponge in the evenings, and I carried plates of food to her in the hope that I could persuade her to swallow some of it.

Days turned into weeks of ritual care, with no visible improvement. I was convinced that if only she could regain her appetite, she would change back to her old self.

I made up my mind to persuade her to eat.

Ómama was dozing on the bed in the narrow room when I entered carrying a steaming bowl of soup. Her left leg was raised high, supported by pillows and wrapped in a towel that made it seem enormous. The rest of her was bundled into a goose-feather *dunyha.*

I brought the soup Grandma boiled for hours on the stove. She made it using the goose bones left over after we had chewed the last bit of meat off. She carefully preserved these in goose fat. We still had some scrapings of the precious fat left because Grandma was very stingy with it, trying to make it last all winter.

I didn't dare to sit down on the edge of Ómama's bed because I was afraid of touching her sore foot, so I stood a step away and smiled at her, trying to see in the dimming light whether she was awake or asleep. Her face was sunk into the pillow, her chin covered by the *dunyha* that belonged to Grandma whom I had heard insisting that Ómama needed it more than she did. "She's stuck in that cold room, poor woman."

The Kendes had several maids before the war. Architects of the time didn't consider the comfort of domestic servants important. They economized on space to the extent that I could hardly turn around between the narrow bed and a small chest of drawers pushed under the window.

As I stood by Ómama on this darkening winter afternoon, I didn't switch on the bare bulb hanging above her bed. I held the bowl in front of her face until she opened her eyes. Her hand was shaking as she lifted the spoon towards her chin. I watched her spill half of the first spoonful on the *dunyha* , but I didn't move.

I cleared my throat and forced myself to talk to her, trying to be her loving and reassuring granddaughter, while all I felt was unease and pity.

This was not the Ómama who used to laugh and tease me, who dressed me up in the dresses she had sewed for me, who took me on prideful walks to Szent István Park to show me off to her friends.

"It is a good goose bone soup," I said. "Grandma sieved out the bones for you. Isn't it good? Or is it too hot?"

"It's fine," she said, but so quietly I could hardly hear her.

The bowl was still half full when she pushed it away and turned her face towards me.

"I have to go," she said. "Will you help me, please?"

She was heavy. Favouring her inflamed foot, she leaned on my shoulder. Apu's flannel pyjamas were too big for her and hung away

from her body releasing an odour that made me hold my breath. We had to shuffle through the kitchen where the new neighbour was chopping onions, a smell I welcomed. She didn't look up, and we pretended not to see her. Ómama most likely didn't need to pretend.

The bathroom seemed far away, beyond the kitchen door at the bend of a long hallway. Ómama needed help to pull off her pants and to take her seat on the toilet. I stepped back and closed the door, waiting outside for the sound of flushing.

No, I was not embarrassed. I felt sadness and repugnance. Repugnance mixed with memories of an Ómama who used to smell of sweet soap and the hyacinths she had blooming in a pot on her windowsill every spring.

When I settled her back in the bed, I felt I could bring up the watch she gave me to cheer her up. I was hoping to offer the leftover soup again.

"I love the little watch," I said.

"What watch?" she whispered.

I leaned closer. "The watch with the gold hands and the pink and blue enamel case. It is beautiful. It has a lovely gold winder, but I can't wind it up. I can open the back and see all the little screws and the spring. It is perfect as it is. Thank you for bringing it for me."

She repeated, "What watch?"

"You know, the watch you had in the suitcase."

"Suitcase?"

"Yes, the suitcase Apu brought it with you from the ghetto. The old suitcase."

"It's not mine." She turned her head towards the wall, but her voice grew stronger with anger. "I had a basket full of food. They stole it."

"The watch..."

"What?" She sighed and closed her eyes.

I picked up the bowl and turned to leave, but the bed creaked, and she reached out and grabbed the edge of my apron. “You look like her,” she whispered.

“Who?”

“The same face. The same age. The eyes.“

“Who?”

She turned her head towards the wall, and her hand fell back on the bed.

128

Ómama's funeral

I am in Rákoskeresztúr on a frosty winter morning.

Stepping out of the cold funeral parlour, I leave behind a crowd of relatives and some total strangers.

I feel offended by them. She was my Ómama. How dare they cry, when I can't cry?

I don't want to let Ómama go to an unknown land. I want the old Ómama back, the one before the ghetto.

Confused, I keep walking in the snow.

I come to a halt in front of a square tombstone. Its top rim is capped with caked-on ice. For a while I stare at the Hebrew inscription I cannot read. With my fists in my pockets, I tremble, not only due to the cold, but to the immense mystery of the blackened writing. I don't know who lies below the stone and what the words mean, what anything means.

Ómama a victim, helpless, old and sick? Ómama in a coffin?

No, Ómama is more. A survivor. She can't be buried. She is part of me. I am part of her. This is all wrong.

She never told me the name of the girl I resemble. But I know now. I am sure. It is the daughter she lost. The girl who is buried somewhere in this same cemetery. The girl she never talked about.

I stop in front of another old tombstone I don't understand. Who lies here? I am surrounded by thousands of the dead around me. My turn will come.

That's it. We take turns.

Ómama is what I shall become. Ómama went to where her parents and all her ancestors are, where I shall go, and where everybody now gathered inside that cold funeral parlour will follow. This must be the order of things. And an order is an order. Unchangeable.

Words swirl in my head faster and faster. I have to grab one, get hold of a handle and hang on. Death, birth, inevitability, darkness, dust to dust, worms, heaven, hell, nothingness, eternity.

I settle on inevitability. I am still shivering.

Ómana is part of an endless stream. So am I. It reaches for thousand and thousands of years into the past and through me, her only grandchild, reaches into the future.

Tears?

I'll follow you Ómama. I know. I am on my way.

I return to the parlour to stand by my father.

The crowd slowly follows the coffin, a straggling line of survivors, black mourners against the white snow. At the gravesite a tall man I don't know sings a heartbreaking lament whose words I don't understand, but his resonant voice makes me shiver again. I close my dry eyes.

Much later Auntie Bella told me what people said about me. "She didn't love her grandmother. Didn't shed a single tear."

129

Walking by the Markó Street Jail

On the first day of school enrolment after the war, when I was finally allowed to attend Ráskay Lea Girls' Gymnasium as a proud Roman Catholic again, Apu walked with me, showing me the way. As a reporter always on the go, he could take the time.

Anyu, the typist, who had found a secretarial job at a trucking company by the Kerepesi Cemetery, was tied to her office desk every day.

We walked along Lehel Street and crossed Váci Road to Csanády Street, turned into Visegrádi Street proceeding towards Szemere Street and my new school. I toted a leather satchel and walked with the dignity of a freshly-minted *gimnazista.* My satchel was heavy with new notebooks bought at a Váci Road stationer and it gave off my favourite scent, the smell of paper and glue that permeated that shop.

As we passed by the massive building of the Markó Street prison with its barred windows, Apu touched my shoulder and slowed down. "Always remember this," he said. "Some people locked up in these cells may be totally innocent."

I watched him adjust his hat and turn up his collar before we walked on. I didn't know what to say, but after that day, every time I happened to pass by that building coming or going to school, I thought about the people locked in their cells whom I couldn't see and who couldn't see me.

I imagined them in rags, skeletal and barefoot, chained to a wall, like people in the medieval dungeons I had seen in the movies. Their image fused with the distorted drowning faces on the bas-relief hanging on the wall at home.

A mother's day

The mother of the fallen soldier
doesn't cry.

Her eyes ran dry.

She stands frozen-faced
by the coffin of her son
draped with the flag of the land
while the cameras are rolling.

She listens to the speeches
of those who dispatched her son:
presidents and generals
clergymen and prime ministers
combatants and acquaintances
extolling his great valour,
praising his sense of humour.

Mother of the fallen soldier
makes her way home
to the house
where he was born.
She stands in front of a sideboard
that holds an oval frame
with a photo
of her son in uniform.

Mother of the fallen soldier
gets hold of the oval frame,
rips out the shot
of her son in uniform,
replaces it with her son
holding aloft a fish he caught,
his first one.

Mother of the fallen soldier
then sits down.

130

Vali and me

Who wants to hear it now?

Vali's story is as close to me as my own.

We met in school six decades ago.

Every time I return to Budapest, we meet again and we talk.

We argue. I want to know every detail of her life, but she is not keen to speak.

Yes, you are right, I say, it's easy for me, living far removed from the carcass of a war whose scent in Budapest still permeates the walls, no matter how many times you cover it with fresh paint.

How did you paint over your mind? Vali responds.

Did I? Did I do that?

Inevitably, we end up rummaging in the past, debating our childhood.

Two armchairs, two women, the same conversations through

middle age into old age. She sits with her back turned to a window, her source of light for many decades, her view through six regime changes.

I face this window looking out on the street where I can see homeless men exchange their loot, fossick in shopping bags filled with oddments they gathered from waste bins, receptacles of litter across the city.

Vali nursed and buried her husband a few years ago. She also nursed and buried his mother before that, and before that she buried her grandmother, who raised her. She knows where they rest. She does not know where her mother and her father are buried, and not knowing how they died is the millstone that weighs down her spirit.

Yes, I say, I can visit the graves of my parents.

Learning odd bits of information through the years didn't help, she says, so I don't talk about it. Who wants to talk about the past any more? And who wants to hear?

Dusk settles over us as I empty my teacup. Vali serves old-fashioned tea in cups and saucers with lumps of sugar in a matching bowl. She doesn't turn on the light. Her white hair shines in the beam of a streetlight that seems to penetrate the room more aggressively by the minute.

Why do you want to know? She asks the umpteenth time.

Yes, I do want to. I feel I need to know in order to know you and to know myself.

Sounds like self-serving curiosity, she says.

No, no.! I protest. It is hurtful to know, but I want to know your mother's story, because it is your story.

My story is the story of millions, she says.

I need to know you because I am convinced that I could be you, just as you could be me, and that by chance, we've led such different lives through no fault and no achievement of our own.

We are not interchangeable, she objects.
By the chance of birth…
You were the lucky one, Vali says.

131

Vali tells all she knows

All right. You want to hear.

Here it is, she says.

I tell you the story of my mother. The parts that I know.

Look at this picture on the wall. That's her. The year before she married my father. She was 18. Only a child. A year later I was born.

I called her Mami.

She was born in Budapest in December 1914, so when she died in January 1945, she was only 30, young, blonde, blue-eyed.

I have her eyes. Her hair.

She got top grades in the *Mária Terézia gimnázium* and set her heart on studying medicine. There were two barriers in her way.

She was female and she was Jewish.

The *Numerus Clausus Act,* the first anti-Jewish law in all of Europe was passed here in 1920. It limited the number of Jews allowed to enter institutions of higher learning.

After many failed attempts to study medicine, she enrolled in a school for shorthand typists, but instead of work, she chose marriage and motherhood.

She funneled all her energies into my upbringing. A gentle

person, kind and quietly spoken, that's how I remember my mother, and that's how others saw her.

Trying to save our lives, there were some Catholic priests who baptized Jews seeking protection.

Ever since her school years which my mother spent in a Catholic school run by nuns, she was strongly attracted to the Catholic faith, and when all three of us were baptized in October 1944, this step did not seem to her an exigency, but a long-nurtured desire coming to fruition.

My father was different. He was older.

Papa was born in 1901 into a poor family with three children. His father, a carpenter's apprentice, was drafted in 1914 and died somewhere on the front in the first year of the First World War. His mother, heartbroken and destitute, died a year later of cancer. The three boys, 18, 13 and 10 were left orphaned. The 18-year-old went to work to support the other two, and the young ones sold odds and ends on street corners to earn some money. They lived alone and managed to stay together, run their household on their own and assiduously avoided asking for help, because they didn't want to be separated in orphanages and foster homes.

I can't help being amazed that through all that, each one of them managed to matriculate and that the oldest one became an architect, while my papa and the youngest became accounts clerks.

My father went to work for a factory manufacturing braiding for traditional coats and uniforms. It was called *Reich és Fiai Paszomány Árugyár.*

He was a very private person, whose life was centered on his work and his family. Although, I must add, that he failed to show openly his devotion to us.

By the time I was old enough to remember, we did not see

much of him because starting in 1940, he was drafted to work as a Jewish labour serviceman.

By 1944, our fate was sealed.

My grandfather was 57 years old when the Arrow-cross men took him from their Csáky Street apartment saying that he was needed to do a "little work in Germany".

He tried to calm his wife saying that he did not mind, "At least I have a chance to see the world now. I've never been abroad."

We didn't see him again.

We managed to get *schutz passes* issued by neutral countries to protect us from deportation, papers that offered a false sense of security. We had to move to a so-called "protected house". We seemed to be moving all the time, and moving meant standing in long lines for hours on wintry streets holding mattresses over our heads, waiting to be assigned a place in a house so crowded already that one hardly could find a space to put the mattress down and go to sleep.

One razzia followed another, and they always took with them some of the people, but they still accepted our schutz passes. Once they grabbed my mother though. They said "for a little work", and took her to the big KISOK playing field, but they released her the next day.

On November 26, a German and an Arrow Cross man combed through the house and when we handed them our passes, they ripped them apart calling them *schlecht,* worthless. That was one of the worst moments of my life.

With a long line of others we were herded down the stairs. At the bottom there was a recess leading to the door of the concierge. My mother suddenly pushed me in there and the concierge grabbed me and took me inside until everyone left.

During the later raids in that house, after I tore off the yellow star from my coat, I would quickly put it on, cover my head with a kerchief, and start down the stairwell by myself. When I was stopped by soldiers, I said that I was only visiting there. They looked at a blonde, blue-eyed girl with a turned-up nose, not at all like a Jewish caricature in their newspapers, and told me to get out quickly. I left and walked around the neighbourhood for a while and only returned when the coast was clear. I wanted to stay there, in case my parents came back looking for me.

A neighbour who worked for the Red Cross thought that a parentless 10-year-old without papers should need help, and she took me to a Red Cross children's refuge on Teleki Pál Street. Here five of us slept on one bed. Then they received a new group of children who were infested with lice.

I decided to run away. I never sewed the yellow star back on my coat after that. When I went back to our old flat, I was not welcomed by the new people who lived there. By then they totally emptied the larder that was originally stocked by my parents and two other families. The only thing left on the shelves was one bottle of vinegar.

That came in handy in the days when there was no longer gas nor electricity and no more water either. I used it to wash myself and I smelled of vinegar for days.

Christmas arrived and the long siege started. When other children in the cellar, terrified by the noise, could snuggle up to their mother, I sat alone. On the 16th of January, just as they show it in films, two Russians entered the house and hugged and kissed our elders. We were being liberated.

Nowadays this word has fallen into disuse in Hungary, and the roads and squares named to commemorate the country's liberation in 1945 have been renamed.

On the 17th of January, grandmother could leave the ghetto and, skirting stacks of frozen bodies, she started to search for me. Among still smoking and burning ruins we moved back into her old apartment. Another family already lived there, but we got along with them fine.

We could not imagine that my parents and grandfather would not come back.

When school started up, I ran home every afternoon hoping to find them there when I arrived.

Grandmother cried every day and kept repeating: "My daughter! My daughter!"

Then slowly the bad news started to arrive bit by bit.

132

Vali's voice gathers strength

My father's forced labour unit was reduced to about 12 servicemen by November 1944. They were kept in the stairwell leading to the cellar in a house not far from us in Budapest.

His next stop was a concentration camp.

He ended up in Mauthausen, and according to several survivors, he was still alive in the last days before May the 5th 1945, when the Americans liberated the camp.

In an article that was published in *Uj Élet* in the autumn of 1945, his name appeared as one of the victims buried in a mass grave on the south side of Mauthausen. To this day I don't know for sure whether my father was present when the Americans liberated the Mauthausen camp, or whether he was among those who were evacuated on death marches from there and herded into Gunskirchen in Upper Austria where, I am told, over 10,000 Hungarian Jews passed through. They could hardly walk. Typhoid and dysentery took its toll.

So is it a mass grave near Mauthausen or a mass grave in Gunskirchen I still dream about?

133

A cry in the dark

Vali's voice speeds up.

She knows the dates, she has each detail engraved in her mind by decades of thinking and rethinking, searching for answers.

On November 26, 1944, my mother and grandmother together with the group led out of our Tátra Street house was escorted to Szent István Park where they were ordered to split into two groups: the old to the right, the young to the left. This is how grandmother ended up in the Budapest ghetto where she managed to survive until liberation. The younger ones, including my mother, were made to march to the brickyards of Óbuda across the Danube. They were kept there with hundreds of others for several days.

I don't know how she managed to send me a missive written on a piece of toilet paper that spoke of her love for me and of her anxiety. She used the intimate nicknames that we always used just between the two of us.

She addressed it to our concierge, and to him she described the terrible circumstances people suffered in the overcrowded brickyard.

Later, when they were herded into wagons, she managed to pass out a similar "letter" on the way. It is lost. I don't know where. I can't find it. I only remember that it said that she was together with a friend, the mother of one of my classmates. A few of the survivors of the Ravensbrück women's concentration camp later informed me that the two of them were inseparable until the very end.

At the beginning of January1945, my mother came down with severe dysentery and typhoid. There was no medicine. No pain killer.

In the last days she cried out. She kept screaming.

"Kill me, kill me! Please! I can't take it any more!"

She died in the arms of her friend who was also ill, and who died the next day.

When I first heard this, I could not bring myself to tell it to anyone, not to my grandmother, not to my uncle. Not to my son.

Now, I am ready. I want people to know her story.

134

Blue eyes

I feel fine as I type Vali's words.

Vali is unwell. Her spine is bent under the weight of years. She suffers chronic pain no doctor can help.

She is living in a society bent on forgetting and even worse, whitewashing a tarnished past.

I live in the Pacific where I witness a drive for clarification, for a frank analysis of the past, coupled with attempts to rectify historic villainy.

Vali's 1944 is different from mine.

How could I match the intensity of her passion to set the record straight?

I know where my parents and grandparents are buried.

I wasn't an orphaned child.

When she roamed the streets waiting for a razzia to end, when she tore off the yellow star and never wore it again, when she had no identity papers, only a peasant kerchief tied over her blonde hair above blue eyes to face the guns, I was ensconced in an air raid shelter and fed by my mother and Grandma.

I could seek refuge in their arms.

135

Toxic utopias

We have been sold so many things through the ages: eternal life in the presence of gods, riches won by the conquest of new territories, breeding an ideally pure society by ethnic cleansing, milk and honey by appropriating the assets of "aliens", reaching Eden by eliminating class enemies and other "traitors", entering Paradise by embracing communism or by turning into clever capitalists.

And when one by one these social utopias turn out to be *ignes fatui,* cold fires, fed by the gasses belched up by the rot of centuries, we try to reignite them for coming generations.

A questionnaire about symbols of veneration

Is it a flower or a flag?
If it's a flower, which one?
Is it a rose? A thistle?
Or a tulip?

If it's a flag, what design?
Red white and blue?
Or yellow with blue?
With a cross? Single or double?
Or with a moon? A cluster of stars?

Maybe it's a tool.
A wheel? A hammer? A sickle?
A sacred sceptre, a dented crown?
Or a weapon of heroic traditions:
an arrow, a shield, a cannon?

Is it a bird? A two-headed eagle?
A bear? A lion? A dragon?

If it's a god, is he wise?
Or jealous? Vengeful?
A sharer of power?
Or does he rule by terror?

Is genuflection still in style,
or are we less keen to kill and die?
Can we see at last
the bloodstained flags of the past
hanging at half-mast?

136

Who owns the past?

An old friend in Budapest tells me that I know nothing and understand nothing about my birthplace because I left and did not share decades of suffering. Only those who share the pain have the vision and the moral right to talk.

Emigrants! Shut up!

He is not alone. Others also think that emigrants and immigrants are dismally ignorant about the place they leave and the place where they land. In between two stools we are supposed to land on the floor. You cannot sit on two at once, they say, and sitting with half a butt on each, you upset the balance and tip over, ending up concussed and confused.

You spout useless opinions. You are a bore. Irrelevant.

You come back to visit the "old country" that in the meantime has changed out of recognition, filled in with new houses, new subway lines, new teenagers and newly abandoned factories. You use your sentimental reunions to show off how well you have done abroad, how you can come and go with ease, how much better off you are than your hosts still stuck where they were born.

How can I answer?

What can I say?

After a prolonged throat clearing, I can say that I go back to my birthplace to pay homage to the land that is rife with memories. To visit the people and walk the places that are dear to me.

And I say that having lived in various places, I have had a chance to compare the various ways of messing up a country and the various

ways of distorting history with self-serving falsifications. Hungary, the land I encountered in my early childhood was a single sample. It was the one I absorbed, breathed in, imbibed in school, the one whose toxins I still can feel embedded under my skin.

I say that the genuine memories of those early years are my own. I see them now more clearly and in context, having learned to teeter on a lot of stools.

I say that I have as much moral right as anyone to scrutinize any place at any time on this small planet.

137

Trembling walls

As a small child, I loved to stare at white clouds floating above me, small tufts of wool carried by puffs of wind crossing slowly overhead. Their silence, their determination to follow each other in one direction without straying out of line, spoke to me of order in the world, of summers arriving at regular intervals, of the strength of predictable continuity.

Then came the war. Tanks. German soldiers.

Then different tanks. Russian soldiers. 1945.

Then there was a pause. The tanks disappeared behind fences.

People made speeches about peace.

Then came a revolution and with it the tanks again.

When the tanks come, the walls tremble. They come one after another with their guns pointing ahead, following so close that they are nose to tail, and they thunder, make the earth quiver and make people move away from their windows, just in case.

There were 11 years between the siege of Budapest and the second siege in November 1956.

When I opened my eyes that cold winter morning and looked out of the window to discover what made my bed tremble, when I saw an endless dark column rumbling along the road, it made me think that tanks mean normality, that peace is only an interval between battles, an aberration, a mere lull, a temporary cease-fire.

War stays crouching in the shadows. Ready to leap.

Acknowledgements

I send my loving thanks to my parents, who taught me to read and write.

Without the help and encouragement of countless other people, more than I have room to list on a page, this book would not see the light of day. They know who they are. When I lost faith and no longer could justify my prolonged hunt for the meaning of my memories, they insisted that they were interested in a childhood spent before and during the Second World War.

I am greatly indebted to Elizabeth Smither, whose advice through many months as my mentor with the New Zealand Society of Authors Mentor Programme has been invaluable. I have enjoyed the support of Paddy Richardson, my manuscript assessor via the NZSA, whose attention and enthusiasm kept me going. I have also benefited from the thorough expertise of Dana Wensley Ph.D. / Pen (NZ) Freedom of Speech Spokesperson and from the careful reading and corrections by Lys Bradley, Denis and Stephen Brown.

Further thanks are due to those who through the decades answered my queries, reaffirmed my memories or sent me valuable materials, including some who are no longer alive to see the finished text: Forgóné Markó Teréz, Budané Nyéki Éva, Korányi Mária, Dr. Varga Margit, Ormayné Cser Vera, Zsoldos Éva, Antalicz Anikó, David Brown, Jozef Peter, Hojsza Zsuzsanna, Oto Pse, Pejo, Kiss Gyula, Ernő Csányi, Michael Gifkins, Singer Olga, Suzi Hume, Hortobágyi Miklós, Halász Éva, Simon Edit, Simon Zsuzsanna, Bodó Manci, Szilvia Szabó, Csapody Tamás, Konrád György, Fehér Ferenc, Imre Kovács, Floria Oliveira, Harmat Zsuzsanna, Paul Maunder, Markó István, Markó Ferenc, Markó András, Markó Robert, Forgó János, Forgó László, Markó Katalin, Markó Lali, özv. Markó Istvánné, Miles and Margaret Jackson, Rita Moran, Akky Leurink, Pam and Trina Sellers, Gurli Hansen, Matt and Carol Harvey, Lynnne and Bill Hume, Heather Lindauer, Lyn Nichols, Bette Norlander, Sara Leach, Barbro and Ross Harris, Barbara Ewing, Chrissie Ward, Joan Harvey, Gábor Tolnay, Shane

Clayton, Max Brown, Ben Hume, Carol Maxwell, Kate De Goldi, Cliff Fell, Paul Smith, Sandy Stephens, Allan and Joanna Innes Walker, Janette and Gerard Hueting, Caroline Selwood, Tig Scott, Eric Schuman, Kornelia Feredoes, Klara Szentirmay, Margot Hannigan, Danuta and Henryk Szydlowski, Maria Farrer, Thomas Pors Koed, Rachel Bush, Jessica Le Bas, Adrienne Frater, Claire and Terry Gavin, John and Muriel Ridland, Louise Gauld, Rozália Bencze, Jane Tolerton, Dinah Priestly, Craig Potton, Vincent O'Sullivan, Chan and Philip Woollaston, Mark Raffills, Gordon and Penny Challis, Mary Thornton and Carol Ercolano.

Without Page & Blackmore Booksellers, Nelson's multiple award-winning independent bookstore, our city would not be the cultural hub of the top of the South Island. Stella Chrysostomou and the whole staff deserve our thanks for their dedication to good books.

I am also thankful to Dave MacManus, Suzanne North and Ro Cambridge of The Copy Press, Nelson, for their competent work and their great support under the pressure of a tight deadline.

Conscience surveillance

From the plateau of the night
the dead are watching over us.
They know what matters,
what is frill or folly.
They know who turns off the lights,
who is true and who is phony,
who rides roughshod over soft grass
and smiles an idiot's smiles
when the path turns to morass.
They know each route we are taking
when we blindly pick the wrong one.
They see themselves anew
when we stumble, rise and rush on
to reach the end
where they doggedly stand
watching over us.

www.ingramcontent.com/pod-product-compliance
Ingram Content Group UK Ltd.
Pitfield, Milton Keynes, MK11 3LW, UK
UKHW041644190726
13854UKWH00006B/2699